Praise for Fra

For most of us a glimpse into a foreign world might prepare us for the reality of going there or reassuring us if having been there we did remember it with some clarity. Survivors of suicide will know the terrain of this experience Missy expertly describes, clinicians who have been privileged to support those on the journey will nod and agree with the words from Jill as they read her analysis of Missy's journal entries. Those who have been fortunate to not go to this other world will marvel at the challenges to survive a bereavement so complicated words can only capture a fog like description of this place of pain and suffering. Missy's use of metaphor can enable a reader to appreciate her journey with images we can relate to even if the pain of this death is beyond our reach with mere words. I know making meaning of suicide loss and providing the installation of hope is the goal of the survivors of suicide I have been privileged to know for over three decades of work in this "Canyon of Why." Reading this book will be a value added to those who have been exposed to suicide and those who will be. Clinicians who read this book will be ready, willing and able to help those they meet along the journey of healing that is so vital in a world where suicide remains so prevalent.

Frank R. Campbell, Ph.D, LCSW, C.T.,
Executive Director Emeritus of the Baton Rouge
Crisis Intervention Center,
Founder of the National Suicidology Training Center
Developer of the Active Postvention Model

During my career as a medical social worker, I worked with survivors and the traumatic aftermath of suicide. Not just another general overview of suicide, Missy's book,

Frantic Unleashed, reveals her day to day, week to week, month to month account of the mind of a survivor of suicide. Her rare raw honesty, vulnerability, and resilience can provide a lifeline to those who are faced with this life changing event. Therapists and those closest to the survivor will also benefit by gaining a deeper understanding of how to best relate and reach out to the survivor.

Bobbie Schultz,
Medical Social Worker, LCSW, NCACII, retired

If there's one thing I have learned from working with those in grief, it's that it is comforting and appreciated when others are willing to share their own stories with raw candor. Missy Palrang has done this. She speaks her mind, her heart, her gut, with love, humor, and rage without censoring herself. The pairing of her journal entries with her later reflections, complemented by observational commentary from her counselor, Jill McMahon, provides a compelling multi-dimensional perspective on the grief process. Many readers will acknowledge elements of Missy's journey as their own, such as the wild fluctuation of emotion, the sense of isolation, the reduced tolerance for petty complaints, or the new spark of fearlessness. Though each experience is unique, readers who have had a devastating loss, particularly to suicide, will recognize a survivor of incomparable pain, and they will accept her full range of response with instinctive compassion—a compassion that is mutually nurturing and reassuring.

Dianne Martin,
editor of the Mornings with the Dads books and You Are Not Alone: Stories of Loss, Grief, Healing, and Remembrance, producer of a forthcoming documentary film about sudden loss and deep grief

As an eight-year sibling survivor, I can say this book beautifully illustrates the crushing reality of what life is for a suicide survivor. Whether you are new to the SOS (Survivors of Suicide) "club" or an unfortunate extensive "member", this book is one courageous woman's journey through the unexpected and devastating loss of her husband to suicide. For those new to their loss, Missy delves into the shock, disbelief, numbness, heartache, and anger that occurs with this incomparable type of grief. For those of us that have been without our loved one for an extended period of time, it allows us to reflect on where we've been and how, just like Missy, we are still alive, still breathing, and still fighting. The book offers what you do not believe is possible in the beginning of your loss and that is hope.

The excerpts from Jill, her counselor, provide a unique perspective from a professional's point of view during this timeframe and information for the survivor or those that want to help but do not know how or where to start. The loss of a loved one to suicide does not define who that person was. The type of grief that is involved is a treacherous and difficult path which coins its loved one's "survivors". The difference from other types of loss is related to the distressing social stigma that still plagues suicide. A change needs to occur. The bravery of Missy sharing her story is one way to shed light on this global issue helping to fortify a change but also to shine a light of why the term "survivor" is attached to a loss by suicide.

Katie Harjes, AGACNP
Survivor of Suicide

Missy Palrang's Frantic Series Book 1 fully immerses the reader into her grief experience immediately following the suicide death of her husband. Authentic and agonizing in places, real and raw throughout, Missy draws us into her world with incredible honesty, gutsy realism, and remarkable self-reflection. Jill McMahon's insight as Missy's professional counselor during her journey adds valuable depth, breadth, and perspective of Missy's grief process as it unfolds day to day. The book skillfully illuminates the reality of grief following a death by suicide.

Lisa E. Schmitt, *Executive Director*
New Song Center for Grieving Children
A program of Hospice of the Valley

Frantic Unleashed

Navigating Life After Suicide
A Survivor's Journal
part 1

Missy Palrang, MS
With Jill McMahon, LPC Grief Specialist

Frantic Unleashed
© 2018 by Missy Palrang, MS
Author: Missy Palrang, MS
Therapist: Jill McMahon, LPC

Published by Sphere4 Publishing
Arizona USA

Cover Photo by: Rebecca Lawson
https://www.bekkilawsonphotography.com/

ISBN (10): 1727464664
ISBN (13): 978-1727464665

The author of this book acknowledges the perceptions and memories in this book are her own and may not be the same for others who are familiar with the circumstances. All care has been taken to protect those mentioned within the books, and some names have been changed. This book contains actual accounts of surviving a suicide. If anyone is struggling with the contents, a list of references where you can get help and support are listed in the back under Resources.

Acknowledgement

An adequate expression of thanks to all who have been part of the team that brought this book to life would require an entire extra chapter. The list would begin with those who were there to pick up the pieces and end with those who've helped bind it up and put it into print…and include a multitude of names in between. There are far too many people to list by name at risk of leaving someone out. Their support has been invaluable.

There are three; however, who were with me before Scott died, were involved nearly as deeply as I was throughout, and are never far from my side today. They are my sister Karen, my boss Neil, and my friend Doug. You guys are the best.

I would also like to send out loving thoughts of gratitude to my brother Mike (d. 05/05/16). I miss you Michael Pickle.

In Loving Memory of
Scott McComb
March 26, 1966 - March 27, 2015

Hole

Numb
Darkness

Despair fear anger confusion
Alone crowded desperate destroyed

She must have

Humility to reach for the hands
Courage to take every step
Persistence to start over
Strength to manage the pain
Love to forgive
Hope to survive
Desire to thrive
Resolve to keep trying
Willingness to bleed

To find

Peaceful excited challenged ok
Joy confidence calm new

Colors
Awake

Whole

Table of Contents

Forward

I first met Missy on March 29, 2015, two days after her husband Scott died by suicide. At that time, I was part of the Phoenix L.O.S.S. Team (Local Outreach for Suicide Survivors). We were contacted by Missy's sister, Karen, and asked to come to her home to help provide support. Missy's friends greeted me and a volunteer team member at the door. I learned Missy is an experienced helicopter pilot, employed as the supervising Chief Flight Instructor at a large helicopter flight school. Many of her peers were present to support her.

We were led through her home and guided to her back patio where she sat staring into space. She was in shock. We answered questions and provided resources. More importantly, we attempted to instill hope in Missy that she would indeed survive this horrific loss. I'm not sure how much she really heard that day. However, I was encouraged there were many sets of ears there to soak it all in. If Missy wasn't able to hear what was being said, I had confidence someone around her did. When needed, they would be there to remind her.

I've been at Missy's side ever since our first meeting. She's allowed me to travel this journey with her. At times she has listened to, and valued, my guidance, and at other times she has needed to carve her own path. At the time of Scott's suicide, I'd been working exclusively with Survivors of Suicide for over ten years. A career I believe chose me, instead of me choosing it. But it's not the degrees I hold, the research I've been involved with, or the seminars I've attended or conducted that have given me the best training. It's the Survivors I've worked with, those bereaved by suicide, who have been the best educators. They are the experts. They live it. They feel it. It is their reality. I've been fortunate enough to hold their hands, listen, observe, and just BE with them when others were too afraid to do so.

The words I share with you in this book are a compilation of what I've learned from others who have walked in the shoes before you. At the end of each chapter, I share with you common reactions, feelings, and behaviors survivors encounter as they walk through the process of healing. When I sit back and listen without judgment, I hear real pain, true sorrow, a little bit of hopelessness, and a whole scrambled mess of confusion. Healing and mending cannot occur until we feel validated and heard…but they are possible!

Just as my notes in this book are subjective to my experiences, so are Missy's. She's come to a place in her grief journey where she feels courageous enough to share her experiences with others. Her journals document the path she walked in the year following Scott's death. Scott was a Veterinarian and prominent figure within their community. Missy chose to acknowledge his manner of death, instead of hide from it. Her observations are raw, emotional, poignant, and sometimes comical. Part One of the Frantic Series records the first three months of her walk, Part Two is months four through six, and Part Three documents months seven through twelve. She makes them available with the hope they will provide some relief and instill hope in those freshly exposed to suicide.

As you turn these pages please keep in mind these are Missy's experiences. Each person will grieve this type of loss differently. For Missy, support groups were helpful in the beginning but later became a source of stress. Others find support groups to be a lifeline. We see in the early months that Missy's anger and confusion presented itself through judgment of others. You may react differently. Missy turned to her faith. You may not. There is no wrong or right way to grieve this loss, there is only your way.

The process of grieving may change constantly. It does for Missy. One thing that has remained consistent since the first meeting is Missy's resolve to overcome this experience. Her focus has always been on living a joyful life once again. Missy will not be defined by Scott's actions. About this, she has always been clear. Together, our hope is that in reading The Frantic Series you will feel heard, validated, normal, and most of all hopeful. If Missy, and the many who came before her can do it, so can you!

Missy had been a client for some time when she approached me with the concept of putting together a book. Her desire to publish stemmed from her wish to reach out and help others who find themselves in the same position as she was…to give them an example of her own survival. I was honored to be asked to add comments at the end of each chapter.

If at any time, reading this book is too distressing to you, put it down. No one says you need to finish it now. You can always pick it back up in a few days, weeks or months. A list of additional resources for support or crisis intervention may be found in the back of each book.

Thank you for choosing to walk some of your journey with us. You are not alone. You will find a strength, deep in the core of your being…a strength you never knew you possessed. Life will be joyful again!

Jill McMahon,
LPC Grief Specialist

About Jill

Jill McMahon is a licensed professional counselor practicing in Scottsdale, Arizona. She holds a masters' level degree in counseling psychology and is a certified member of the National Board of Certified Counselors. Jill began working with those bereaved by suicide in 2003 while working at the Wendt Center for Loss and Healing, in Washington D.C.

Jill works to ensure Survivors of Suicide have access to the available resources. In addition to providing one-on-one counseling, she is a L.O.S.S. team associate, helping to train communities nationwide about the importance of providing swift and sensitive response to families immediately after a suicide has occurred.

When not working directly with bereaved families, Jill is passionate about educating others on the uniqueness of this grief. Her speaking engagements include presenting locally, nationally, and internationally on suicide-related topics including prevention and postvention. She has trained other mental and medical health professionals, Survivors, first responders, church groups, and school districts.

Chapter 1

The First Week

I will want to take away your pain
but instead I will sit with you
and teach you how to feel it.

Brene' Brown

Looking back:

I see in this first week a woman who feels responsible for the broken eggs lying on the ground that someone else purposely dumped. She's confused and trying to figure out how the eggs came to be broken. Her thought processes are scattered and illogical. She frantically tries to restore the eggs to their original condition in their original basket. She has a lot of help in this fruitless endeavor in the form of people she already knew in some capacity, and new ones who have run to her assistance. She sees this broken basket of eggs as an event that has forever damaged her comfortable life, as well as the future she was anticipating. For that reason, she feels intense anger toward the person who dumped the eggs in the first place.

What I know now:

"A load of shit has been handed to you," my sister declared. She was right. You have some difficult work ahead, and everyone around you knows this, but please hear these things…

1

- You will be OK.
- You will feel Joy again.
- You will love again.
- You will play again.
- You will giggle again.
- You will meet some amazing people along the way.
- You will do everything you used to do, if you choose to.
- You will probably do more than you used to.
- You will feel like yourself again.
- You will eventually not even think about this day at all.
- Really, it's true. I've been there, done that.

March 27, 2015 – The day he died. Friday.

The journaling didn't begin until three days after Scott died, so this day is written three years later. It's what I remember about the day he died. I'm not someone who's good about remembering the specific days, times, and even years certain events occurred. In fact, I usually had to consult the engraving on my wedding ring when someone asked how long we were married. But this particular day, month, and year lingers like a scar.

I was eating a hamburger and tater tots with my boss at Sonic Burger Drive when my husband ended his life. I have not been back to Sonic since. When we got back to work, a man and a woman approached me in the parking lot as we got out of my car. My boss later told me he could tell there was something serious going on, so he walked away to give me privacy. They were detectives. I remember someone saying, "very bad news" and the woman told me Scott had died. I think she told me it was a suicide without me asking, or maybe I did. It's all a haze.

I remember calmly walking to her car and sitting there emotionless for the three-mile drive to my house. I remember it was a little car with a dark interior and I felt cramped and folded up inside of it. In hindsight, I just don't think I understood what had happened. The dogs were barking when we got to my house. It's not where he killed himself. Maybe I crawled through the doggie door to get in. The detectives wanted to know if we kept a gun. I checked the closet where it should have been. It was gone. The magazine had been unloaded. I guess he figured he only needed one bullet.

It was my gun from when I was a parole officer. I was very fond of it. The detectives wanted to know who they could call to come be with me. I couldn't think. I finally asked for a friend who lives down the street and my boss. He's a friend also. I wanted him to bring his pastor with him. The woman detective told me Scott had left a note on the kitchen counter. He wrote I didn't "deserve" this and he hoped I could get a "fresh start." He also stated the VA would need to be notified and, oh by the way, make sure to mail a check to the IRS by April 15. He gave me the combination to the safe as well as instructions for getting into our storage unit. He signed it "Scott." There was no warmth in the note.

I ended up crouched in a four-foot space between my bed and my closet. My friend Vicki arrived and sat on the floor with me. Neil, my boss was nearby. I remember feeling comforted by the pastor who was sitting against the adjacent wall with his legs sticking straight out. I think I asked "why" a lot. I was worried about the dogs and wondered how he could leave them. I worried about making it on my own. I worried the blue sweatshirt I was wearing would always remind me of this day. It's one of my uniform shirts, so I told Neil about my concern. He said not to worry, we'd throw it away and get another one of a different color.

I remember thinking people would pity me and worried I would be a burden to them. I was worried the house was a mess and everyone there would notice. Someone handed me a stack of brochures explaining what I might be going through, and about local services to help me deal with this situation. The detectives rattled off detailed instructions about how to proceed with arrangements.

I still hate those brochures; never read them. I threw them away and have no idea what the detectives said about arrangements. The woman said she would be there for me through the process and invited me to call her any time. She never returned my calls. I guess they had to check all the boxes and move on to the next in line. Fortunately, my friends listened and later were able to guide me through the process.

Late that night my sister flew in from Spokane. I remember the first couple of hours after it happened but have no memory of anything for the next eight hours or so. I remember my sister walking in late. I was sitting on the dog beds against the living room wall. The room seemed full of people. Sitting on the floor became my comfort zone in the months to follow. She just sat down and hugged me. There really was nothing to say.

March 30, 2015 – Three days after.

My husband Scott chose to end his life three days ago, the day after his 49th birthday. The aftermath is beyond comprehension for me and everyone else who loved him. So much to do, I don't even realize what needs to be done. I'm so sad and angry, mostly angry he would leave me in this position. I can't really even focus on the pain he must have been in, or the how or why. My focus is on me and the immeasurable ways he changed my life by doing what he did.

Didn't it occur to him I'm not properly equipped to take on all the things he did around the house? Didn't it occur to him he was my daily lunch partner? That my weekends which revolved around him were going to feel very empty now? That I have no one to travel with anymore? Go out to eat with every weekend? Go to movies with? Be silly with? Have inside jokes no one else would "get"? That he was the only person I felt ok being around without make up? That I don't even know how to provide medical care for our five pets? That his dogs would miss their dad's presence? That Baby Cat won't have his warm tummy to lie on in the middle of the night? That he was my emotional support system? Didn't he understand when he destroyed his life, he was destroying mine as well? Except I'm still here to try to put it back together.

I love him and appreciate him now more than I ever did when he was alive. I should have been more supportive, more loving, more something. Of course, everyone says only he is to blame and "he's made the choice" and "we can't control other people" blah blah blah. Well to them I say: Of course, I could have been a better wife so don't tell me I couldn't have stopped this. You don't know. No one knows for sure, but it makes them feel better to say that with the hopes I will believe it... Maybe in time.

Mostly right now I'm angry. Angry he, without my consent, turned MY life into something I don't recognize or want. I liked my life, it was good, it was our life. Happy, purposeful, full of future. Now it's just empty. I don't know if I feel more loss for what I had, or loss for the future we planned. The trip to Colorado Springs next month, the trip to Greece in July with my mom and sister, all the travel that was such a big part of our lives. Just the daily being together and scheming about our retirement plans and how we need to work hard now to stay physically and mentally fit so when we retire in seven to ten years, we can still be active. I haven't sorted that out yet.

He was my everything, my other half. We were one of those couples who did everything together. Maybe he just wasn't as happy with our life as I was. Maybe this was the only way he had the courage to escape it. Why didn't he just ask for a divorce if that was the case? Why didn't he reach out to me? To anyone. Or maybe he did, and I didn't recognize it.

The little things are the worst so far, things no one could understand. Sitting in church yesterday with my sister on one side and my friend Randy on the other, it hit me hard that if he was there, I would be leaning against or physically in contact with him in some way. Yesterday I was sitting by myself.

Listening to the conversations of all the wonderful people who have taken it upon themselves to fill my home in this time. Enduring the comments, they have no idea absolutely tear me up. Telling me stories about places they've been. Yep, been there…when he was alive.

The little things… Four new rose bushes bloomed simultaneously for the first time…we had been looking forward to this day. It's here. He's not. Doing the laundry, washing and folding his clothes that were still in the laundry like normal and wondering why. What's the point? Just walking through the house where every single little itty-bitty stinking thing is a part of our story.

Everyone thinks I'm a "very strong person." I'm not, I just have a big mouth. He was my support. He handled all the hard decisions, conversation, and situations. What I was able to do was only because I knew he would pick up the pieces if I failed. How do you move forward? Can I ever recover from this to have a happy full life? Right now, it feels like not. I can't imagine if he knew how much he was taking away from me, and his family, and his co-workers, and his clients, and this world that he would have done what he did. Why didn't he know? How did I fail him? How did we?

March 31, 2015 - Four days after. Tuesday.

Everything is a reminder. Things people say affect me in ways they don't understand and shouldn't be expected to. Hearing someone say "My husband..." is one of those things. It hurts tremendously. I don't have one of those anymore and guess I didn't realize how much I loved saying those words when I did. I should have appreciated those little things more. It's so many little things. "We this or we that." There is no "we" anymore. I have to get used to saying "I" or "me."

Driving by the golf course and being reminded I don't have my golfing partner to go out with anymore. Even though we had stopped golfing several years ago, it was always an option. It was always in the future as part of the retirement picture. That looks a lot different now. The mention of a certain restaurant we used to love and go to nearly every weekend. How do you go out to eat when you're alone? Friends have their own lives and besides, it's Scott I want to go with. He was always my first choice. The traveling we had planned together. We were so perfect for each other in the things we liked to do.

Our weird sense of humor no one understands. Our adventurous eating habits. How can I still be me if there is no him? Did he really understand how much of my life he was taking with him when he chose to go? How could he not see I'm not equipped to handle this life without him? We were a team, codependent on each other to survive. What gave him the right to change my life beyond recognition? Maybe he didn't see that.

8

I met with the financial advisor and accountant yesterday. Fortunately, it's not grim. Of all the other "shit that has been handed to me", as my sister puts it, this one should be ok. One of his life insurance policies had just expired and the new one we set up to take its place was less than two years old. Either way both are invalid. It was a lot of money and it would have helped.

Banking...not my strong suit. Karen and I met with the banker to verify accounts, balances, etc. They need the death certificate. Hard to hear. The oh-so-kind banker Sarah, who is 25 years old, lost her brother when she was 17. Her advice to stay in the moment and not worry about the future seems so wise coming from someone half my age. She remembers worrying about Christmas, his birthday, etc. She said just deal with those days when they come. They will be hard, and it will get easier although you will never forget. She shared with me that for a week before her brother's birthday, she spent every day worrying what that day would be like.

Today I bumped into a Fed Ex delivery driver who delivered to Scott's clinic. He told me how sorry he is. The far-reaching effect of this act is immeasurable. So many people affected in a horrendous way. Would he have done this had he known? I like to think not. Returning home, I found a dog food receipt in the back of Scott's truck. He bought dog food two hours before he did this. Did he know at that time? Was he trying to make things easier for me? Did he REALLY think two fucking bags of dog food would make this easier in any way? How could anyone do this to another person. In my head over and over and over... How?

April 1, 2015

Everything is a blur and out of order at the moment, nothing fits together, makes sense or seems to stick. I asked my sister if my words that don't seem to flow smoothly are a result of the medication she's given me. Probably just the stress and "fog" the counselors said would occur.

Scott's counselor John agreed to meet with me with the understanding he could not talk about Scott. I understand but having a connection made meeting him easier. So kind, generous, and totally sincere. He said when he heard, he closed up shop and went home for the day. I'm so sorry, John. Ironically sad, but funny, story is he accidentally overcharged Scott last time, so I got that refund. Who goes to a counselor and makes money? Additionally, he did not charge me for this session because he cared for Scott too. I'm overwhelmed with his honesty and compassion. He will see me a couple of times but then wants to refer me on to someone who was not seeing Scott. I'm disappointed but understand.

Mostly I cried/sobbed during my time with John. I told him I was angry. He said I have a right to be. Scott took something from me without my consent or permission. I said I had a good life and he destroyed it. John says it's not destroyed, just different. I don't want to be someone who attends counseling and joins a group called SOS, Survivors of Suicide. Who would? I can't imagine being a member of a worse group. He said, "Don't call it that, call it the group for very angry people who were left behind and

10

have to deal with it." Much needed moment of levity. I told him I know why Scott liked him so much.

Karen stopped by the veterinary clinic where Scott worked to find out if it's ok for the dogs to keep going there every morning. It's their routine. The staff, she said, are wearing orange and black ribbons for him. I guess for the colors of his alma mater. The dogs have been a big part of the clinic for as long as we owned it (10+ years) and even after we sold it. The dogs "Nurse Brittney" and "Assistant Coco" would accompany Scott to work every morning and stay in his office or in the reception area. After Brittney passed away, sweet little Brownie became Coco's "assistant." They were part of Scott's team, anxiously awaiting the word every morning that it was time to go to work. Karen was told the dogs are a part of Scott the staff would be grateful to continue seeing. I'm grateful for this so the dogs can have some normalcy in their lives. They were definitely daddy's girls.

Penny to the Rescue came to visit. I met her in the women's bathroom at church a few days ago when my friend Randy took my sister and myself on Sunday. Randy has been so kind to bring my favorite convoluted Starbucks drink nearly every morning. Takes a real man to order half water, half soy, five matcha, one peppermint, and light ice. He's a cop though so he can and does deal.

Randy was visiting also. He told me when he stopped by the clinic to pick up Scott's things, the staff asked if they can keep the deer heads he has mounted on his office wall. WHAT??? WHAT???? I always assumed they tolerated the heads. But want to keep them? And "the Pig."

A 3'x5' ceramic pig Scott surprised me with on my birthday one year. We saw it in a gas station/truck stop at Picacho Peak driving home from my parents' house in Tucson one day. After laughing with our completely dorky sense of humor about how funny it would be to have it in the house, I distinctly remember saying, "But DON'T come back and buy this!" Seems somehow the word "DON'T" bounced off his head while the other words crawled right into his brain. With the help of his friend Mark, the life-sized adult pig ended up in my living room towering over the normal sized furniture. We painted him just the right color of pink. It took two tries to get him right. The next Christmas a giant rooster showed up. Still have the rooster in the house but the pig moved to the clinic to be a center piece of doggie day care. Allowing the heads and pig to stay at the clinic was approved with the option to recall. The staff also asked if I would return a birthday card they gave him the day before he did this. I'm not ok with that so it stays with me.

Anyway, back to Penny to the Rescue... It's the most unpredictable things people do or say, or events which cause the sudden onslaught of tears. Memories, sadness, the moment when you realize yet another plan for the future has been crushed. Anger floods that he's not here to be part of this. This time it happened at church in the moment when I was sitting in my own little isolated box instead of leaning against Scott. Didn't even make it past the opening music and the women's restroom was the closest cave I could find to crawl into.

I was sitting on the couch in the bathroom crying when someone sat next to me and put her arms around me. She asked if she could pray for me. She did. I blubbered and blurted to her what had happened. I missed the service but what Penny gave me that day was much more valuable. She's a gift and a blessing. She took the initiative to put her number in my cell phone and mine in hers. How is it possible this unbelievable woman walked into the bathroom at just the right time and did just the right thing for me? When I finally looked up and my eyes were dry enough to see through the tears, I saw she wore a name tag. Penny. She's a greeter at the church. She wore a shirt that said, "To the Rescue." Penny to the Rescue. I read it out loud and began to laugh at the irony. Penny definitely came to the rescue.

Of course, she followed up and came to visit my house. She's just that kind of person, a sincerely loving, kind, caring human being. She told me about her family, her husband's new job adventure, her fall and broken arm from an over-sized bike in the middle of a parade. She invited me to join her family in Flagstaff for a zipline adventure. There is no way she could have known, nor did I, that her generous offer would be a complete stab to my heart. I'm a homebody. If I was going to do something like that, I would want to do it with Scott. Not with a happy family to remind me I don't have one anymore.

How do you deal with these things? You can't just not talk to people. Most of the time talking is a great distraction and comfort. Sometimes though, a lot of times, one innocuous thought, one word, or one conversation is just too much, too much of a reminder. There's no list you can give someone of taboo topics. There are too many and you don't even know you've found one of those topics until it's too late. I guess you just have to live with it and understand it's difficult. Stay in the moment, as wise Sarah from the bank suggested. I've really been trying to follow her advice, but sometimes it's the in-the-moments that are the worst.

Today also included working on the autopsy and funeral arrangements and all the crap that goes along. Cremate? Bury? Who the fuck cares? The information they need, his social security number, his VA discharge papers, how long have we lived in Arizona? And where before that?

In a sick and sad way, organizing and planning is a safe zone. It's surreal and I'm just part of the team making the arrangements, doing my job like I do at work every day. It's not a personal situation for me. I'm the planner, the organizer, the one who has the big picture and makes the small parts work together but gets to stay in the background. But then reality. It IS personal. This is Scott, my husband, the person who was so much a part of me that I don't know what do without him. The person who chose to end his own life and caused mine to veer to a new trajectory I don't want to be on. That person who made me a Survivor of Suicide. That bastard I love and miss so much. It's very personal.

April 3, 2015

One week. The passage of time has not eased the pain and despair. On the contrary, yesterday was the worst of all. Only a short time of the day was spent not in complete desperation. Even the constant presence of friends in and out of my house did not make a difference, just a suffocating blackness. Impossible to break away from. The situation is what it is. Nothing can break the feeling of no light at the end of the tunnel or anywhere to be seen. Neil's wife, Jennifer and I attended our second "Survivors of Suicide" meeting. Hate the name in case I've not mentioned it. One of the families had lost a son. The mother, father, and sister were all there together and I wanted to scream... at least you fuckers still have each other. I have no one. No family in the area.

Therapist's reflections:

Suicide is known as the act of taking one's own life voluntarily and intentionally. The term historically applied to this act is "committed suicide," and it's the term Missy used in her early entries. It's what she knew, and to maintain the authenticity of her journal, the content has remained unchanged from the day it was written. However, this term - committed suicide - can be offensive and hurtful to many of those closest to the deceased. The friends and family left behind are termed Survivors of Suicide, and you will see that term used in this book.

"Committed" carries with it a negative connotation, suggesting a crime or a sin occurred. Survivors can feel as though the world is judging their person when they hear this term. They already feel as if society is judging the manner of death, their family dynamics, etc. Use of the term "committed" can be painful and cause additional separation and isolation for the Survivor. Survivors are

15

faced with not only their grief but with the pain that comes with feeling judged. "Died by suicide" is now the term used by mental health professionals and most Survivors of suicide.

In addition to this judgment, one of the distinct differences between this loss and others is the social stigma associated with suicide which isn't present with any other loss. Much like a homicide, or a fatal car crash, losing a loved one to suicide is sudden. The grief is intensified. Yet, losing a loved one to suicide is different than other sudden losses. It's loaded with shame and guilt. It's this shame and guilt that makes a Survivor feel misunderstood and alone in their pain.

Because this grief is unique, and our support systems often don't know how to respond appropriately to help the Survivor, the Survivors are left to try to maneuver the depths of this loss on their own. It's not uncommon for those bereaved by suicide to isolate themselves.

Just think, prior to your loss to suicide, did you and your family discuss suicide? Were you raised in an environment where suicide was looked at as weak or selfish? Would you have known how to help someone through this loss? Would you have been comfortable mentioning their loved one's name weeks after the death?

What I notice during the first weeks following a death by suicide:
- Most often shock and denial have set in. This is the brain's way of protecting the Survivor. Shock and denial are a gift!

- Although Survivors are fully aware of the death, they can simultaneously be experiencing denial. The reality of their situation has not yet set in. They can't seem to get dressed alone. They could go days without eating, and honestly would forget their own middle name, in the days after the death.
- Their grief is doled out in small, manageable, doses. Feeling the magnitude of this loss all at one time would be too overwhelming and could be a danger to the Survivor's mental and physical well-being. Once again, shock and denial are a gift.

What I noticed in Missy during this time:

Missy was a hurt, shoulders slumping, confused, stunned, woman in those first days. She attempted over and over to make sense of a situation that never really makes any sense to those left behind. She appeared disconnected, yet coherent enough to know it was important for her to relent and lean heavily on those around her. She was accepting of help. Accepting this help would be valuable for the journey ahead.

Chapter 2

Three and A Half Years Later

Sometimes the heart sees
What is invisible to the eye.

H. Jackson Brown Jr.

July, 2018

It strikes me as notable what I see when I look through the little oval window at the earth 30,000 feet below. In many ways, it's like looking back at my life three and a half years ago. My husband, of nearly 24 years, put my life into a violent tailspin. He chose to take his own life. Distance from his suicide, just like distance from the earth, offers a wider view, a bigger picture. There are no clear boundaries. There are fewer details. The kaleidoscope of color and overwhelming stimulation is absent. The ridges are gentler and the valleys less deep. It's peaceful.

It's a time no longer difficult to think about. It's fresh in my mind as I sit here en route to Portland to meet with Scott's aunt. I haven't spoken with any of his family since July 6, 2015. That was the day when, in a rage, I slammed down the phone while talking with Scott's brother, cutting off all communication with his entire family. Maybe I'm going because I feel I want to explain. Maybe because I feel I need to apologize for cutting her off. Maybe, like the distance from the earth below, distance from that time has changed my view. The reason is not clear to me but I'm

18

sure I'm doing the right thing. A month ago, I sent her a text asking if she would meet with me. She agreed.

Hindsight

They say hindsight is 20/20 but I don't think so. It's not even something we see with our eyes. It's just something we know, sometimes not even knowing how we know it. It's that intuition we're all born with but so carelessly or unknowingly dismiss at times. We recognize intuition with our heart and soul. Most of the time, we've seen it for much longer than we've allowed ourselves to acknowledge.

What I do recognize is the fact I've been given opportunities to participate in things some consider unique. I never thought about it much until one evening years ago, when I was out walking and stopped to chat with a neighborhood couple. Although we had waved in passing on many occasions, I had never spoken with them. On this evening we stopped and chatted for about 25 minutes during which time it came up in conversation that I was currently employed as a helicopter pilot, had been paid to play basketball in Sweden, and had worked as a parole officer for over eight years. Honestly, I typically avoid discussing any of these things but in this perfect storm of a conversation, all three came out. After I hesitantly mentioned the third point in answer to one of their questions, I got a sympathetic look of "yes dear, of course you were..." followed by their shared knowing eye contact and mutual unspoken agreement it was time to end the conversation with this pop tart.

I'm not oblivious to the fact many people are helicopter pilots, or have played basketball in Europe, or were parole officers. However, I do agree the combination of all three is uncommon, and to some, not all that believable. Good thing I didn't mention I have a Masters Degree in Counseling, conducted polygraph examinations for a while, had a lung collapse six times in six months, and am an FAA Designated Pilot examiner.

I've never really had a plan, things just always seem to fall in place. I didn't purposely set out to do any of these things. Each one seemed like a good idea at the time, or the next step on some unknown path I blindly followed. Some people would say I was lucky and some would say I was just in the right place at the right time. Yes, and yes, both are true. But nothing is truer than the two things I now know for sure:

First, God was preparing me for a situation He knew I would encounter. I can see now how those unique circumstances in which He placed me, the people to whom He introduced me, and the challenges He gave me, were finely orchestrated and woven together for a purpose. He was giving me the tools and the pool of strength to deal with a situation that would not just put me on my back, but reduce my life to ashes, a place of darkness. One that at times did not offer even the tiniest pinhole of light.

Several months after Scott died, a friend gave me a piece of jewelry inscribed with Jeremiah 29:11, *For I know the plans I have for you declares the Lord, plans to prosper you and not harm you, plans to give you hope and a future.* Hmm, funny how this fits.

Second, even before my husband's suicide occurred, I was a complete mess. I was merely a list of my titles and achievements with absolutely no idea of who I was or where I was going. Inauthentic, judgmental, empty, and lost, I blindly wandered through life with no meaningful direction or purpose. I was contained in a self-constructed box defined by the labels pasted to the outside. Change, possibility, creativity, and growth did not exist within my box.

My husband's suicide dumped me from my box. It occurred when I was 50 years old and felt exceedingly content and comfortable with life and my list of titles. I was married to an amazing man who was the rock of our marriage. He did most of the work without complaining. He encouraged me to be whomever and whatever I wanted to be without judgment. He was loved by his work associates and clients. Scott was that strong, tall, handsome All-American man, who seemed to have life by the tail. Until March 27, 2015, when he caught everyone around him, me most of all, by surprise and took his own life.

One of the loudest labels on my box said PLANNER. My brain immediately began making a plan to do something I was good at - create order when there was none. What follows is a result of my process. Another label said FIX THE WORLD, so I decided to write a book so others who suffered the same experience would have a plan as well. This shows how illogically I was thinking at the time. First, there is no plan to get through this process, just similarities among Survivors. Second, the plan I laid out for myself, and the resolution I hoped for, definitely made me feel happy and joyful, but more so it made me recognize the wrongness of my box in which I had been living.

I later figured out being violently dumped from my box was just the push I needed to begin seeking something different, something more. Something beyond my narrow definition of joy. I needed to start thinking outside the box. Certainly, there are gentler ways for the push to occur. Life happened. I believe it pushed me in the direction of finding and pursuing my soul's purpose. I learned there was actually a better version of joy than the one I sought to regain. Who knew?

Chapter 3

The Second Week

Friendship isn't about who
you've known the longest.
It's about who walked into your life
and said
"I'm here for you"
and proved it.

Unknown

Looking back:

In this week I see the woman looking at the broken eggs on the ground and feeling devastated, then peaceful, then fearful, then overwhelmed, then in control, then not in control. Restless, panicked, anxious, encouraged, hopeful, sad, insecure, helpless, angry, strong, weak…emotions all coming at her rapid fire and changing at a dizzying pace. She's being asked to make decisions she's emotionally incapable of making. Instead of making careful and informed decisions as usual, she just listens to the options presented to her and picks one, any one, it doesn't matter.

She has to learn new skills necessary to fix the eggs. Fortunately, friends and family have rallied to help her with this endeavor. There are others who didn't pay attention to the basket of eggs when they were whole who are suddenly interested in them now that they are laying in pieces on the ground. She feels obligated to be gracious but sees their attention and desired involvement in the same way she sees those gathered to watch the clean-up of a train wreck.

What I know now:

- You might feel hesitant to ask others for help.
- They want to help…sincerely, they do. They don't know what to do in this situation either. Allowing them to do something helps both of you.
- Even if you're against medication, consider it if prescribed by a medical professional. It's temporary.
- You will have good moments, don't question them, just give your mind a break and go with them.
- You will spend a lot of time thinking about the future you feel you've lost. It's hard to hear this but remember, it's the future…you don't know what you expected would have actually come to pass. You can't lose something you never had.
- You will worry about what people think of you, maybe that they blame you. This is normal even in the best of circumstances. Unless you're the genius who has found a way to control the thoughts of others, let it go. You have enough to think about without worrying what others are thinking.
- People will be unconvincing when they tell you "you'll get through this." Don't worry, even though they don't really believe it themselves, they're actually right. You will.
- Pretty much everything, everyone, every situation, will remind you of happier times. It's crushing but will eventually pass. Hang in there.

- You will have to make difficult choices. Honor yourself first with those choices.
- The opinions of others are less important than they might seem in the moment. Do what is right for you.
- You will find yourself grasping onto anything to return your life to what it used to be.
- Find an individual counselor who specializes in working with those impacted by suicide. It's worth the investment.
- Support groups can be valuable too, depending on you.
- If you have a willing friend, ask him or her to attend the groups with you.
- If you have a Higher Power, lean in.
- If you don't, seek one.

April 4, 2015

A very rough morning resulted in a trip to the Urgent Care with two kind neighbors. A woman from around the corner has been someone to wave at when Scott and I walked the dogs in the evening. She would walk hers, smoking her cigarette. We would wave and comment on the weather. She lives with two other ladies. Oddly I always thought, but never verbalized, I was going to end up being friends with people in that house.

I learned her name is Diane. She dropped a card by earlier in the week which shared the loss of her partner four and a half years ago. She taped it to the front door because she didn't want to disturb me. I also learned her partner's name was Sandy. They'd been together for 20 years. Her letter expressed understanding of my situation and extended an invitation to call her cell or home any time. The time to call came very quickly.

This morning Karen had to go to the airport to pick up our brother Mike who will stay with me when she leaves tonight. Having her here has made all the difference but didn't stop the dark times. The attorney in her knows how to organize and move the ship forward. The sister in her knows what to say, when to say it, when to listen, when to encourage.

I was in meltdown, so I called Diane very early, waking her up. Her friend Cheryl, who is Sandy's sister, decided medication would help me cope and Urgent Care would be a good place to get it. Long story short, I ended up with something to take during the day as needed and something for the night to sleep. Really hard for someone who has always been anti-medication to go for this plan. But the day pill seemed to help.

Afternoon and evening were mild on the meltdown (as I've begun calling it) scale. It was time to have the "when to return to work conversation" with Neil. He has been an unbelievable support from the very first day. Most of the hard tasks and details have fallen on his shoulders. He dealt with the autopsy, the examiner's office, a special blood test Scott's family wanted to test for a gene they believe can cause or contribute to depression, getting his ring back for me, urn selection. He was even kind enough to arrange and pay for a plumber when, by Murphy's law, the guest toilet broke.

Neil also agreed to take my dogs Coco and Brownie to sniff the body. Scott always believed animals needed to see and sniff the bodies of our deceased pets to fully understand and move on. Otherwise they would always be searching. Karen went with him and sat with the "box" Scott was in while the dogs sniffed it. She told me she felt "Scott was gone" and the dogs sensed it too. I hope he's still near me. I want to believe he's here giving support, understanding the grieving, holding my hand. And happy, I hope he's happy.

The "when to return to work conversation..." As expected I continue to have "Princess Status" as Neil has reminded me for years. His graciousness and willingness to work me back in slowly is overwhelming. My feelings of embarrassment over what happened and how people will see me are unfounded, he says. The when and how to return is undecided. A couple of hours per day? In the evenings when most have gone home? Weekends at times no one is there? Bottom line, I'll return when I'm ready. We both agreed my task and goal-oriented personality will do better with getting back to it sooner rather than later. Fortunately, my office has a private bathroom for private meltdowns in the event of such an occurrence. My only request is, in the beginning when I'm there, I would like Neil in the office as well...a security blanket. He has no problems with my request.

April 5, 2015

Nine days since he left. It's Easter. The last day and a half have been oddly and frighteningly serene. It can't be this easy. Relatively speaking, of course. But the unexpected moments continue to be so difficult to handle. Yesterday, during a walk in the park with a friend, she pointed out a lovely tree. She couldn't know the aspen tree is my favorite. But Scott knew. One more of the many things only he knew about me. One more innocent comment that takes my breath away, tightens my chest and ends in tears. Just one more reminder our 27 years together is gone and can never be replaced.

But today, finally a glimmer of hope for a productive future. A friend from California visited. We discussed resurrecting plans for the non-medical home care business Scott and I were set to launch in a few months. Without Scott's skills, I was at a loss how to proceed. Cheryl, a soon to be retired professor at a college of veterinary medicine, has the interest and ability to step in and become the missing part of the business. Whether it actually happens or not, it at least made me think I could have a happy and productive future. I didn't see one before her visit. Did God open this door when he closed another? If it never comes to pass, it at least provided hope.

I visited Randy at his farm then went to Easter Service with his family and my brother. A beautiful happy family is hard to see. This week church was more manageable than last, when I spent the entire sermon in the bathroom with Penny to the Rescue. I made it through today but had to sit for much of the standing part. The medication? The low-calorie intake? The stress? Maybe I just never liked to stand for the music in the first place. So I sat. It was ok. No judgment.

The ATM machine… A wonderful contraption. Stick a card in and out pops cash. Scott was my ATM. I told him I needed money and there it was on my dresser. I carry everything in my pockets instead of a purse, so Scott, knowing I like large bills to minimize the bulk, usually left me three or four larger bills. Apparently, the ATM dispenses only twenties. I feel embarrassed to know so little about it. Guess I'll have to adjust.

Spoke with a woman today whose husband committed suicide seven years ago and left her eight million dollars in debt! Yes, eight million. Her name is Jan, Scott's aunt introduced us. She's gotten it together and is now "happier than I've ever been." First "survivor" to say that…so encouraging. Finally, nine days after the fact, there's a light. Someone telling me with authority I'll be ok and joyful again! Today has, for the most part, felt normal. This certainly has to be the calm before the storm. Right? The meltdown has to be near? The reality? The deafening silence in the house that is yet to come? The loneliness? The not having a built-in lunch partner, movie buddy, travel pal?

They say the first of everything is the hardest. The first Easter… one down, many to go. Sleeping pills kicking in…

April 9, 2015

Stopped counting the days since it happened. The last few have been a whirlwind of planning and general avoidance to everything. The sleeping pills allow for mostly restful nights but it's still not unusual to have a couple of hours awake, when the ugliness climbs through the walls and infiltrates my brain. Reading helps usually. Reading novels now is impossible but short bible verses or inspirational books work.

My days are marked off in terms of appointments. Friends coming to visit or running to the rescue when I can't figure something out (what to do with all the mail that looks like bills but really isn't, how to turn off the pilot light in the fireplace, etc). Meeting with the Pastor who will do the service. The non-stop medical/health appointments, very difficult for someone who doesn't like, and rarely visits doctors. The new primary care doc fortunately referred by another doctor friend. The individual counseling and support groups full of survivors banding together to "heal." Feels like an endless array of appointments that wouldn't be necessary except for…

I'm not a social person but oddly, having all these people in my house hasn't been horrible. I guess it's better than the other option of a silent house. It's funny how priorities and comfort levels adapt when you're in survival mode. I'm a clean freak (not a neat freak, clutter is ok). Scott was very tidy. My brother who's now living with me is not. Oddly enough, I don't care. I just dust the crumbs off the couch, remove and rinse the dirty milk jug from the recycle bin and put it back. I don't even care about the condition of the bathroom he's using. His presence far outweighs any of the mess but makes me realize how good I had it with Scott.

I met with Jill, the SOS counselor, a couple of days ago. She and one of her leaders came to my house a couple of days after it happened. That's what they do, come to the rescue. Then she met with my friends and family to explain what to expect and how they can help. Can anyone really help? Not even sure what she told them, I kept having to leave the room. It was too much. I do remember her saying I was lucky to have so many people sitting in the room. She told them their job was to be my "bubble wrap". Some people have only one or two around them to support them. That's not a lot of wrap. It's sad.

I shared my concern with her about being so peaceful for the past couple of days. I'm worried I've pulled out every defense mechanism known to man but will eventually fall off a cliff at the end of the road. She says it's ok for now. The mind finds ways to protect itself and dole out small pieces of pain at a time. She would be worried though if this continues or "flatlines," as she called it.

In my head I see a huge pile of dirt dumped in the middle of my road. I can go around it and pretend it's not there, or I can grab a shovel and scoop away one shovel full at a time to get to the other side. I choose the shovel. But for now, I'm not scooping. I just glance at the mountain ahead of me occasionally, then deal with the immediate situation. It will still be there when I'm ready to start digging.

The service is in two days. It didn't become real until my friend Vicki and I talked about it and she said, "when you walk in…" That's real. I have to attend this monster I'm planning.

People will be staring at me. I'm the lady whose husband committed suicide. They'll feel sorry for me. I don't like to be the center of attention, and I certainly don't like to be pitied. We decided it might be best if I walk in with my family at the last minute, right before it starts. Dilute the attention. A herd of his family will be descending on Arizona, so it will be easier to blend in. Twenty-two of them I've heard.

Received an email from Scott's mother which said, "I trust there will be an opportunity for sharing from the people assembled…since those who show up will be there because of something special that brings them. Since we know so little of his professional life we are eager to hear from those who are moved to be there." WHAT??? I wanted to scream, maybe you could have visited him all those times he asked you to. Maybe you could have picked up the phone to call him more than on his birthday. Maybe you could have at least said hello when he called you and only his dad would speak to him. Maybe a month ago, when he called to say he wanted to fly to Oregon to visit you, you should have encouraged the visit instead of saying it wasn't a good time because you were too busy planning your own birthday party…and you needed to "clean your desk." Maybe you should have shown a little interest in seeing the clinic your son built from scratch and was so proud of. Maybe you could have spoken with some of his clients who adored the ground he walked on, you know, "those who are moved to be there." But you didn't. Now, it's too late. This isn't your funeral to plan, it's mine.

But I didn't say any of that... I just didn't answer the email.

Also, during the meeting with Jill, I told her about the conversation with Cheryl, about moving forward with the home care business. Not a good idea right now she said. Focus on you, deal with this. That can wait. She's the expert and I'm trying to do as she says but it's difficult. I'm a planner, thinker, doer. I need to have goals.

And then...there was the unannounced visit from Scott's uncle and his wife...

I was having a good conversation with Vicki and her mom, looking forward to the arrival of a great friend, Kim. We were besties in grade school, living blocks away from each other, having sleepovers on either her or my family's trampoline, eating salted rhubarb from her mother's garden, having swim parties at my house with her in her cute little girl bikini and me in my cut off shorts and tee shirt. Riding her pony Smokey down the street, trick or treating as Paul Stanley (her) and Gene Simmons (me) from KISS. We lost touch after high school until six or seven years ago when she moved to Arizona. I'm grateful she did and happy to have her back in my life. We're lunch buddies now with a relationship you can only have with someone you've known since childhood - the history, the stories, the shared experiences during the formative years.

When the doorbell rang Mike got up to answer it. I assumed Kim had arrived with the Greek lunch she promised, so generous and thoughtful of her. Nope, not her. Instead, the uncle and wife walk in with exaggeratedly long faces, barfing sadness all over one of my rare moments of numbness. Sometimes I forget others are grieving too. I'm not the only one suffering.

Vicki, my angel and bulldog protector took control of the situation and explained that as soon as Kim arrived, she was taking me to Costco. All true, although we had planned to eat Greek first. I knew switching Scott's Costco card into my name was going to be too emotional to handle on my own so I asked Kim to help. Everyone needs an explanation. I get about as far as "he passed away..." before the tears come and I'm unable to speak.

Kim arrived and explained to uncle and wife we need to run to Costco. Uncle says, "Do you mind if we follow you?" I said, "Oh do you need to go to Costco for something?" He said they did. The wife looked confused and said, "We do?" I thought, whatever. I said, "Sure no problem." He wanted to buy some nuts.

Off we all went to an experience one might only see on a Seinfeld episode. The uncle stood in the typical Costco line with his basket overflowing with one single can of nuts. Only when he got to the front of the line did he realize you actually need to be a member of Costco to make a purchase. Uh, its COSTCO? Kim gave him my new card to use. Something about that can of nuts sitting all alone in the oversized basket was very fitting.

April 10, 2015

It's the day before the service. I went to the church today to "see the layout." It was Neil's idea - I'm glad he suggested it. Walking into the empty room made everything so final. Reality hit. This is the place we would *do the deed*. Put the period at the end of my husband's 49 years on this earth. All the distracting planning is over. It's time to pay attention to this nightmare that feels like it will never end. Brief moments and even hours of reprieve still lead back to the same reality. He's not coming back. There's no future for us. The plans we had are not going to happen. It's just me now. Being surrounded by family and friends serves as a distraction but doesn't change the fact he's gone. I'm grateful for the distractions but still aware of the reality.

Family has begun arriving in town. Twenty-four of his family and three of mine... The dysfunction bared wide open. The parents who've not had much to do with their son for years suddenly taking an interest. Being told by Scott's brother his parents should not be relegated to the third row at their son's funeral. This upset me. They've been too busy doing their own thing for the last ten years, uninterested in even walking into his "church" and now they want a front row seat? Then there's the first cousin who lives within ten miles of us but only called when he needed advice on pet care yet wants to attend the "friends and family" reception after the ceremony. Really?? Do they think we've all gathered for a fucking reunion?? Same for the "second cousins twice removed" who've never been even the tiniest part of our lives. All now posing as "friends and family." It's very hard to swallow.

Then there's the eulogy I'm supposed to write by tomorrow. I've had over a week to work on it and have gotten as far as exactly nowhere. Kimmy saves the day. Not only did she gather my sister from the airport today, but she sat with me for about an hour asking questions and taking notes, so she could write the eulogy. An amazing save when I really needed it. Again, friends taking care of things for me in ways I never imagined. She'll send it by tomorrow for me to proof and finalize.

Karen arrived in the evening, back from Spokane where she lives with her family. I'm so happy to have her back and wish I could keep her forever. Obviously, that's not possible.

Therapist's reflections:

I spend much of my time educating others on what makes a loss to suicide different, unique, traumatic. It boils down to two simple things: guilt and shame. Did I say simple? There is nothing simple about carrying the load of guilt and shame on your back.

Blame is very much a part of both of those things. Many cultures struggle to grieve in a healthy way, but Americans take the cake. Embracing loss, allowing others to mourn, really truly mourn, has never been our strong suit. We view tears as a sign of weakness. We certainly don't know what to do when someone hasn't returned to their "old selves" within a few weeks. As with mental illness, the stigma surrounding suicide often causes others around us to become so uncomfortable they would rather be continually stung by a bee than to be in our presence long term.

However, the ability to lay blame, point a finger, or find some sort of answer tends to calm those around us. It's not uncommon for extended family members, neighbors, and friends to create a story about suicide. "Well, I heard she was in an abusive relationship, that's why she did it." Or, "I've suspected for years she was cheating on him. Poor guy." What about, "He was obviously addicted to drugs. That's what happens." Yes, these things have actually been said.

Those around us are simply trying to explain what we soon realize is unexplainable. I call it the "Not my family" effect. In some cases, by blaming someone, or something else, they are shedding their own feelings of guilt and placing them elsewhere. Typically, this is a phase of denial, and it doesn't last long. Eventually these individuals will do their own grief work, and it's just as painful as the work you are doing now.

For those outside of your immediate circle, laying blame or deducing a cause is a way to dispel their internal fear that suicide could happen in their homes, to someone they love. Suicide is the scary boogie man you watched in the movies of your youth. It's viewed as a shadow looming. There is almost nothing more frightening. Our culture has allowed it to be, by not talking about it.

As I have said many times, and will continue to remind others, you don't know what you don't know. Until you've experienced a loss specific to suicide you cannot begin to comprehend how complex it is. Don't spend time trying to educate others - especially not at this phase. Maybe later, when you've recovered some, when you've patched your gaping wounds. For now, find your ear muffs and focus on keeping yourself alive.

What I noticed in Missy during this time:

Shock and denial were taking up space in her home. They would come and go, sometimes only visiting for hours, and other times staying up and partying into all hours of the night. Sleep was a real struggle for her.

Missy was always waiting for the other shoe to drop. She would rob herself of any momentary relief (even if it was very brief) obsessing over what painful thing would follow - much like Wile E. Coyote awaiting the anvil to drop on his head. This was a loop repeating itself in her grief over and over, and it's not uncommon for most Survivors to experience the same.

Chapter 4

The Third Week

Courage doesn't always roar
Sometimes courage is the little voice
At the end of the day that says
I'll try again tomorrow.

Mary Ann Radmacher

Looking back:

In this week I see the women with the broken eggs beginning to recognize, yet not quite believing, the permanence of her situation. She's beginning to panic and beginning to seek help from resources she previously shunned or even mocked. She's trying to make living life as "normal" as possible her priority, and resolving the broken egg situation as she is able to fit it in. But her life isn't the same normal it used to be. The broken eggs aren't going away. They haunt her and scream for her attention almost constantly. She's trying to formulate a plan to restore the eggs but has lost confidence in her own abilities. She seems to be wandering down roads leading nowhere.

What I know now:

- You may lose confidence in yourself, even with things you're good at. It's ok, keep trying. Even little successes will put you back in your comfort zone for a while.

- Your brain will be on overdrive as it tries to repair itself. Thinking, thinking, thinking all the time. Let it run, it's doing what it needs to do to heal.
- You will attach meaning to things that previously had no meaning to you.
- Just about everywhere you look, you will read things, hear things, see things that are helpful to you in the healing process. Carry a notebook to record and remember those things.
- Your reactions to situations around you might be very different than in the past. If you can, consider why you reacted as you did. But don't stress about it.
- Remember, you're going to be OK!

April 11, 2015 – Day of the service.

What a morbid, numbing, and final day. There also were times I laughed. It's hard to consider a service for someone who committed suicide to be a "celebration of life." More like a "look what you did you fucker" day. The service was scheduled to begin at 3:00, so at 2:30 my sister, brother, mom and myself packed into the car and plodded forward. Today was the first time I saw my mom since Scott died. Uncomfortable, I felt like I needed to protect her. We left the house later than we hoped but I guess they couldn't start without me.

Eleven friends and family I wanted around me during the service met in a room to the side of the chapel. It was the perfect group. I'm so grateful they would all be with me at this time. A photo montage of Scott's life was showing in the auditorium during the seating. I asked for it to be turned off before I walked in. I was not ready to see them.

Eleven of us lined up, I was second in line, Vicki was in front of me and Karen behind. They were my training wheels. I was shocked to see the 500-seat chapel overflowing to standing room only. I was filled with pride for Scott. Friends, family, his staff, clients, our gardeners and housekeeper, my coworkers, and others whose lives he had touched...all there. Although I didn't want to look anywhere except at the seat reserved for me in the front row, I made myself look. The front of the church had tons of flower arrangements... Tons. I think there was also a box up there somewhere containing his ashes, I definitely didn't look at that.

The service went as I had hoped. I actually felt like we'd put something together Scott would be happy with. I had heard the military would be doing a flag folding presentation, so was expecting it. What I didn't expect was that Taps would be played as a part of the ceremony. I think it was the most difficult part of the entire thing. Something about that music… I don't know where the folded flag ended up after I handed it off to someone. I'm sure it will make its way back to me eventually.

The speakers were my brother Mike, Scott's brother Peter, his co-worker Dr. M., and his fishing/hunting buddy Hunter. I don't remember if I asked them to speak or if someone else arranged it. Regardless, they all touched hearts. I remember sitting there thinking, how did this happen? How could this get past all 500 people in this room? Why didn't someone stop it? This shouldn't happen to anyone, especially him. So many people he could have reached out to. I feel guilty. What did I miss? What did I say that I shouldn't have, or not say that I should have? Others have expressed the same thing.

I'm so angry with him for purposely bringing the blazing aftermath of his death into our lives. Who would do that? I'm sure he didn't realize, but he should have. Hopefully with time, I can feel less anger, and focus more on the 27 good years. Right now, it seems impossible. Anyone who has ever felt suicidal should be required to spend a week with someone whose loved one committed suicide. The more recently it happened the better. They should be forced to see how it absolutely destroys the lives of everyone else, or at least makes them completely unrecognizable.

It had been my plan to get up and walk out the side door without speaking to anyone after the service. Halfway through, I decided they were all there to show respect for Scott, so I needed to show respect for them. It was a long, hard walk up the aisle to get to the back of the church, but it was the right thing to do. I think I was out of my seat and half way up the aisle before the pastor finished saying amen. I didn't like everyone looking at me and I tried to stay invisible by hunching in and keeping my head down. I stood by the door saying thank you, shaking hands, and hugging people for about 45 minutes… Or maybe it was 5.

Neil and Jennifer hosted the reception in their lovely home where we all enjoyed chatting and eating delicious BBQ. Isn't that what you're supposed to do at a "celebration"? Eat and be merry? Fuck that, I just wanted to sit in a dark corner and eat the brisket and beans. I'm not a crowd person and it was always easy to hide behind Scott when we had to do events. Nowhere to hide anymore… it suddenly occurred to me.

Scott's family made their glorious entrance with their ever-present drama. Most people there probably didn't notice, but I did. Everyone always seems to be upset with someone else. Since Scott and I were on the outside, they all confided in us. The sister in law doesn't like the mother because she forced her husband to wear a kilt, and she calls the husband's sister "10-Key Eyes" …says whenever she walks into the room she begins calculating how much everything is worth and how it compares to her stuff. Yes, it's that ridiculous.

I spent my time around the "friends" part of the "friends and family" with an occasional brief interaction with the "family" component. Scott's side all just pretended to be one big happy family. I hope to maintain a good relationship with his family, but don't want the drama. Besides, with him gone, they may not want to maintain a relationship with me anyway. Scott was always happy with our decision to move states away to avoid this exact problem.

April 12, 2015 - Day after the service.

Keeping busy helps me avoid thinking too much about this new and unwanted situation I've been shoved into. I'm angry that someone who was supposed to love me put me in this shit hole. Mostly I wonder if I'll ever recover from it. It's weird to be so angry and so sad at the same time, about the same thing.

I met with the accountant today to discuss what exactly I'm supposed to provide to him every month. He showed me the amounts I have to pay for the state and federal taxes. What the hell? Who has that much money anyway? Hopefully, I do. It's not even like we have to pay it, it's just me.

Being alone in the world after having the other one here for 27 years is a feeling I can't begin to explain. Friends, neighbors, family are all great support, but at the end of the day I feel like it's just me now. At the end of the day everyone else has their own families and lives to go home to. Having my brother living with me for now is a luxury. I know I'm fortunate. Many in my situation end up going home to an empty house. Like a woman who loses her baby during birth and goes home with only a blanket.

Somewhere in this two-week nightmare, my in-laws expressed to someone that they didn't know a lot about Scott's life. You think? Perhaps paying attention or showing some interest may have solved that problem. Just a thought... So I reached out and asked if they would like to see our house and the clinic we built from scratch. Yes of course they would. I showed them, painful detail by painful detail, every part of our house and Scott's space. His closet, his hunting gear, his beloved fruit trees, the carpet/paint/tile/cabinetry/etc. we had chosen and installed over the years. The birdfeeder he had just hung outside the bathroom window so one of our cats could watch the birds, his office where he did all the bills and paperwork, the couch we sat on every night watching TV while we ate dinner.

At the clinic, same deal. The special ceramic toilet paper holder we purchased in Oregon for the client bathroom, the office with a bathroom we designed especially for him, his pride and joy deer-head mounts, the birthday surprise pink pig. I described how we picked the colors, how we designed the layout, and how we decided which services would be offered at the clinic. Everything. We hugged and went on our way. Hallelujah, they now know how their son spent most of his adult life, working his ass off to achieve all he achieved. The funeral ceremony already showed them how much he was loved.

April 13, 2015 - First day back to work.

I only stayed for a couple of hours. Karen went with me to "see the office." She was really babysitting me, but I didn't want everyone to know that… They probably did. I showed her around at a time when I knew many of the instructors would be there. Mostly just to get the awkward gawking out of the way. It was uncomfortable, I feel like everyone is thinking "there's that lady whose husband killed himself." I don't want co-workers to feel sorry for me, but I know they do. Karen was kind enough to sit in my office with me for an hour while I did a bit of work. She brought a book to read.

What I was afraid would happen, did. I had a very hard time concentrating and kept making silly mistakes with a task I was working on. It was a simple calculation, but I kept putting the wrong digits in the calculator. That's not normal for me. A couple of the instructors ventured by and nervously said hello. I tried to set the tone, but it seems they're as nervous about being around me as I am being around them. I heard at the service, there were a bunch of them sitting in the back row who gave up their seats and stood when it became standing room only. I'm so proud of them for doing that.

Karen and I met with an attorney today. She's an attorney also and thinks there is some way I can recover some life insurance, which as of now, I'm not entitled to. We were in the middle of changing Scott's policy and put a new one in place 10 months ago. It has a 2-year suicide exclusion. Swell... My life has become like a shelf lined with Cracker Jacks... "*a prize in every box.*" Sometimes I'm sad he will miss out on so much of the future we had planned. But things like this make it very hard to feel sorry for him.

April 14, 2015

Karen left today. It's so much harder without her here to direct traffic...and to talk when I want to talk, when the tough times come up. It's all the little things that cause constant tough times. Seeing our beautiful and shy cat

46

Baby doing something cute that only Baby can do. Thinking, "HOW COULD HE LEAVE THIS BEAUTIFUL CREATURE?" Seeing the new hunting boots he so proudly picked out last Christmas, just sitting in his closet now. Opening the other closet and seeing the camo jacket my parents gave him. Every time he wore it he said, "I LOVE this jacket!" He loved the deep pockets. Seeing my dirty car sitting in the garage and remembering how diligent he was about taking it to the car wash for me. He surprised me with the car and took pride in keeping it clean. He even went out to the garage with a spray bottle and rag just to "touch up" the wheels. Everywhere I turn, every little aspect of my life, is a constant reminder of him. There is an ever-present dark shadow over my life now that just doesn't go away. Crying comes so easily.

I've taken a lot of comfort in my Christian friends and the books they've given me. The daily passages I read always seem to be written specially for me. Jesus Calling has been my favorite. Two people gave me the book so I'm saving one to pass on to someone else in need should the time arise.

I spent a couple of hours at work again. This time by myself. For about the first hour I just sat there staring at piles, moving them around...nothing accomplished. Neil came in and we talked about a new student orientation he had attended. Normally I do those. It was good to talk about work, although I didn't really contribute. One of the instructors came in and asked me a couple of questions I was actually able to answer. Finally, a little bit of normal and a little bit of accomplishment. Five minutes out of two hours.

Neil sent me a text in the evening that said, "Very nice to have you back in the command chair today!" It made me feel good to hear that, but my response was, "Thank you I didn't feel very in command, but I can pretend." Neil is not like most bosses. I think he'll give me space and support to work toward productivity slowly. I have a job to do and want to do it.

Something unexpected happened when I decided to watch TV for the first time since that day. Scott and I always ate dinner on the couch together, watching one of our favorite shows…Survivor, Amazing Race, Blacklist, anything food or travel related, and our latest obsession, Walking Dead. Never live, only recorded so as to skip through commercials and maximize the amount of TV we could squish into the evening. Sadly unproductive, but true. From the long list of recorded shows, I chose Survivor so I could discuss it with a coworker tomorrow. It's our routine. Something normal. I put dinner on my tray, sat down and hit play.

What I did not expect was the complete lack of interest I had in watching. I love the show but couldn't focus enough to maintain any interest in it. I turned it off after fifteen minutes. I was trying unsuccessfully to recapture a routine I had with Scott. Watching our shows was such a big part of our lives. I hope this is a temporary thing. I don't really feel sad or mad about it, just stumped. I didn't expect it to happen as it did. I thought, if anything, the sadness of watching without him would be the reason I would have to turn it off, not lack of interest.

April 15, 2015

The illustrious real first day back to work. Going in with Karen a couple of days ago was just practice, a test run. The brave drive to work fell apart at Starbucks when I walked out with my 3000 calorie, $15 dollar cup of sugar and whipped ice. It happened when I saw a penny lying on the patio. Finding stray coins was one of our "things." Scott was better at it than I am, although it didn't matter who found what, we would both feel as giddy as two little kids splashing around in a mud puddle. It never mattered how much money we had or didn't have, we still would have the same excitement over even one penny.

Seeing the penny on the patio was just one more reminder that he, and any future moments like that, were gone. Sadness flooded my head and then poured out my eyes. I considered turning around and going home but I sat in the parking lot for a few minutes taking deep breaths, and then continued.

Locking my door and working from within the safety of my office with no interaction was the best option for today. Much of the time was spent crying in the corner, or in the bathroom attached to my office. I texted Neil and told him to just come in if he needed something. Into the office, not the bathroom of course. He did a few times, which were the less crappy moments. Being able to strategize about work situations like we usually do, provided a comforting feeling of normalcy, something that's so absent these days. I want to get back to my routine but it's hard to concentrate. Nothing feels important. I can't say I achieved really anything today. Neil knows, although he doesn't let on.

One of the hardest moments was receiving an email from a dear friend in Sweden. Daniel is the younger brother of a girl I played basketball with for six months. He was a very young, innocent, wide-eyed, nervous boy when he lived with Scott and I in Tucson for three months fifteen or twenty years ago. He's grown into a wonderful, adventurous, mature, young man who I love dearly and am blessed to have in my life, along with his partner Jimmy. His email was heartbreaking. He, like everyone, does not understand how this could happen. How do I even respond?

Neil invited me to go to lunch with him and Jennifer and one of her co-workers. I felt like the third wheel everyone feels sorry for. I know it's my problem. They certainly didn't feel that way… Or maybe they did but I don't think so. They are very kind people, I'm the one with the hang-up.

The SOS group was a large one tonight - about 14 people plus the facilitator. It struck me as terribly sad there is such a need for this group, that there are this many people committing suicide. How many more are there not attending who should be? The leader said the Phoenix area averages two suicides per day. Sickening. It's not the one destroyed life I think about, it's the dozens of other devastated lives around each suicide that is mind boggling.

Don't they know what it does to their loved ones? Don't they consider us? Or do they? But make the choice anyway? It's impossible to know - impossible to understand the upheaval in every single aspect of one's life that is changed forever when someone takes their own life. I know I'll never be the same. I try to convince myself I can be as happy as I was before...but I'm not very believable. The "new normal" everyone says. What a dumb term. I don't want a new normal, I want my old normal.

In group tonight, the sharing was too graphic for me, I had to step outside. One of the members was describing viewing the body. I missed most of the story but heard enough. Too much. Now I have an image stuck in my head I don't want there. It's why I chose not to view his body in the first place.

The leader joined me outside for a moment and I told him about the Starbucks penny and about my first day at work. His son died about six years ago. Suicide. Now he volunteers his time to the organization which provides free groups all over the valley. The same group I designated as the "in lieu of flowers" organization.

Tonight, I realized I need to bring a notebook to the group because the members have such awesome words of wisdom. I want to remember them all. One of the ladies has a similar attitude as mine, "it's not going to define me" she said. Me either. I got her number after class and am going to find a way to get to know her and learn more about her experience. Her husband killed himself over a year ago. She seems happy. Amy is her name.

Finances are another area causing me extreme stress. My sister has looked at what I have and is confident it will be ok. I've never had to pay bills, never watched our bank accounts, never even thought twice about spending money. It was just magically taken care of for me. Now I worry about every little dollar and wonder if I should be saving it. We were two earners, I am one. Maybe getting through a few months so I can see the in and out will help me feel more confident. I'm so unprepared for this shit.

April 16, 2015

Second real day back at work. I would like to say this day went better but it didn't. Same problems as yesterday, just worse. I listen to Joel Osteen (JO) on the radio whenever I can these days, he gives me hope. Oddly enough, I had just started listening to him about a week before Scott did this. "Did this" is about the best I can say most times; the other words are too real and descriptive. This morning Joel was talking about being compassionate and encouraging to people. I wish I was more of those toward Scott. It just tears me up inside to think how I could have treated him better. How I could have been a better wife. He was so talented, loving, and thoughtful but I didn't tell him how impressive I thought he was. I should have been more positive. More compassionate and encouraging. But now it's too late.

Lunch at home today was difficult. Scott and I had our routine of meeting to eat out most days. It was a time to relax during the middle of the day. I meet friends occasionally, but he was always my first choice. With the two of us, there was no need to pretend, entertain, or even talk sometimes. Just be together. He was not a great communicator. That was hard for me. I like stimulating conversations involving contributions from both parties. I commonly felt I was doing all the work and he just listened. Sometimes I felt bored, like my brain was not being challenged by any new ideas. I would get angry with him and tell him that. What a bitch.

Mike was here when I got home. When I was peeling an egg, I dripped egg slime on the counter. I felt angry and cussed. Mike loudly said, "What now?" On top of an already crappy day, and having to eat at home, his comment threw me over the edge. I burst into tears and went outside to eat my salad. I know he didn't mean any harm. I just couldn't handle his comment, at that moment. Everything sets me off. I tried to compose myself, then explain to him how every single detail of my life changed when Scott did what he did. How I'm trying to maintain a small part of the life I used to lead. How this includes keeping things clean. How being criticized for trying to do that was just too hard to take. How there is so little I can control now.

He apologized and said he was just trying to be sarcastic and funny. I told him right now very little is funny to me. I also told him I am "so, so, so" glad he's here and hope he isn't going away anytime soon, but to "please try to understand how those comments affect me." He says he does. The truth is, unless you've been the leftover from a suicide, you really can't understand.

Another comment hard for me to hear from him was when I told him I'm reducing the number of sleeping pills the doctor gave me. I've never been a pill taker and don't want to be now. It's not me. His response was, "Why not take them, everyone else in the world does." Again, not the right thing to say. What I really wanted to hear was something like "How can I help you with that?" Being questioned for what I do, or why I do something is really difficult right now. It's hard enough to make decisions without being second guessed.

Amy and I are scheduled to have lunch next Monday. It was hard to reach out but I'm glad I did. First impressions could be wrong, but I think she and I are going to click. I feel like a taker though, she has so much to offer me, mostly her wisdom of making it this far. I have nothing to offer her.

Tomorrow I plan to begin meeting with the pilots and trying to engage again. In other words, open the door and let people in.

April 17, 2015

I made it through my shower without crying this morning. First time since that day three weeks ago. Perhaps I was too busy making a mental list of all the things I now need to do in life – and trying to wrap my brain around how I can do them... Before, there were two of us to share them, now it's just me.

My to do list:

- Stay physically healthy - Eat right, sleep enough, get back to exercising, start getting routine medical exams, figure out a new health insurance plan – my old one was through Scott's work.
- Get emotionally healthy - Keep attending groups and individual counseling, seeing friends, talking about his decision and the aftermath.
- Get spiritually healthy - Attend church, continue my readings, keep talking with people, maybe join a small group. This is number one, but I didn't think of it until third. Just shows how far I have to go on this one.
- Take care of my two dogs and three cats. Feed them, walk them, vet care, love on them.
- Earn a living. Keep working and start to figure out a way to do my home care business.
- All the other stuff. Pay the bills, keep the house clean and orderly, yard care, do the banking, and so many other things that keep popping up and shouting "don't forget you have to do me now too!"

As usual I was in tears by the time I arrived at the office. My plan is: arrive at times when I know the fewest people will be between the front door and my office, keep my glasses on and head down, walk straight to my office, shut and lock the door behind me. It worked again today, got the door closed with no one seeing me. After about an hour, I decided to crack it open a few inches hoping no one would want to come in. No such luck, business carried on as usual. I was quickly back in the swing of the daily coming and going of instructors with their questions. Being able to answer them made me feel useful.

Everything was going ok until Randy stopped by. I was telling him about a message from Joel O. this morning and the waterworks started up. Again. So unpredictable, so frustrating, and always at moments when I least expect. I also told him about a different moment from earlier this morning, the sheet incident...

I suggested to my brother he change his sheets today, so he would be on the same schedule as Zilda, the cleaning lady. This way, she could wash his too. He argued. I bit my tongue. He brought them to me in the laundry room. Solved, right? Not even close.

Something about seeing him carrying our sheets, mine and Scott's, was unbearable. Those are our sheets and we should be sleeping on them, not him. So...off to the bathroom to cry again and to try to come up with a plan. I decided I would buy some new ones and explain how I feel to him, then hope he would understand. At lunch later in the day, Vicki suggested I wash the new sheets and lay them out for Zilda like normal. Genius. Mike would not need an explanation and would never know the difference anyway.

Then there was the Osteen incident. On the drive to work I was listening to Joel with one half of my brain, and mulling over the sheet incident with the other half. I heard him say the words, "From ashes rises beauty." Scott's body was cremated, a decision I never in a million years thought I would have to make so soon in life, and certainly not so suddenly, without any forewarning. But it turned out to be one of the few decisions I could actually make with clarity in an otherwise foggy world. Nearly all of the others fell to my sister or someone else. I physically couldn't open my mouth sometimes, or even think when someone asked me a question. Hearing Joel say the ashes thing was such a wow moment - in good ways and in bad. Bad because it was a reminder of the place I find myself in, good because it provided hope there is life after the "ashes." For both of us.

Tomorrow is a neighborhood garage sale and I know Scott had planned to get rid of a lot of things. I'm not sure what he had in mind, and I'm certainly not ready to sort through things to figure it out. I do know he wanted to get rid of a twin bed I've been hanging on to for years, thinking we may need it someday for a bigger house. Yeah, as if that's ever going to happen now.

Two items to sell. Woohoo, big garage sale. At least it will go quick. I don't want the neighbors to think selling those items has anything to do with what he did. I've asked my brother to sit out there with me, so I don't feel awkward sitting by myself. It wouldn't have phased me before. It does now - maybe because I don't want the neighbors to see me sitting there alone. I don't want them to feel sorry me.

It occurred to me, tonight marks the end of the third week of a very long nightmare. I've had good moments and even hours but so far, no days that felt normal, peaceful, or in any way secure. On the contrary I feel completely unsure of myself in every aspect of life. It's a 180-degree change for me.

Security unraveled is a frightening and lonely feeling. No longer is that special person here to rely on, go play with on a whim, dream about the future with, talk about our shared past with, giggle with about private jokes that have become ours over 25 years together, assume will take care of me when I need taking care of, "trade rubs" with while we watch TV every single night on our couch, text silly pet pictures to every day, and know will be on the other end of the line when I call. That person is not here anymore. Driving home tonight I had the weirdest thought, I thought, he is nowhere on this planet, not even on another continent. Even my Swedish friends are there, and I know it. Even if I don't see them for months or years, I know they are here…on this planet. Scott is not. Nowhere. There is nowhere I can drive, fly, walk, or sail to find him. He's just gone.

Therapist's reflections:

When someone dies you feel your future has been taken away. It's as if you've been robbed at night while you slept, unsuspecting. Not only do you mourn your loved one, you mourn the future you envisioned with them. The future you now know you will not have.

When you're young, you visualize your life's story. You begin to draft your goals and dreams. You imagine what your family will look like, where you want to live, and what you want to accomplish. Each phase of life is like a chapter in your own personal book. You work for years to make this vision of your story come to life.

When you lose someone suddenly, traumatically, it's like the final chapters of your book have suddenly been ripped out. The ending you had written is no longer applicable. What happens next? You spent your lifetime drafting this novel, and now what? Survivors have to re-write the last half of their book. You are left to reformat your story, even if you did not choose to. But first, you must stand still. Feel, ponder, develop a plan. Then you can start an outline.

I was training a group of Social Workers at the Phoenix Veterans Hospital several years ago and speaking about the intricacies of suicide grief. Toward the end of my presentation, a kind, older, gentleman from the back row piped up and said something like: "You've spoken so much about the emotional and social challenges Survivors may face after a loss, but you haven't mentioned the financial stressors the sudden loss puts on a family, and the pure mental exhaustion of trying to figure it all out." Oh my goodness, he was right! He and I spoke for a long time afterwards, he educated me on how stressful maneuvering the financial aftermath of death can be. He lost his wife months earlier and was knee deep in legal documents, bank statements, and a tangled mess of red tape. It's a part of this grief rarely discussed or rarely given any credit for our distress. However, financial stress is absolutely real. It's a new, and unwelcomed, guest in this life after death.

What I noticed in Missy during this time:

Missy became frustrated with her lack of concentration and was desperate to be in greater control of her mental faculties. A feeling of worthlessness came along with this inability to be her old self. Feeling as though she couldn't perform as she used to, Missy blamed herself for letting others down, only to repeat the pattern again the next day. Missy's expectations of herself were unrealistic for a woman who just experienced a sudden loss to suicide.

She held on tightly to those voices who comforted her. At this time, it was Joel Osteen. She was contemplative and worked hard to find good in messages meant to be motivational. She worked hard to be present to positivity. It was not easy.

During this time, find your Joel Osteen. Maybe its Oprah, or Maya, or Deepak. Maybe it's the neighbor four doors down who you've only spoken to three times previously. Hope and compassion can present itself in the least likely places. Find yours.

Chapter 5

The Fourth Week

You will find that it is necessary
to let things go;
simply for the reason
that they are heavy.

Unknown

Looking back:

I see the woman with the broken eggs slowly gaining clarity and confidence as she navigates her situation, only to be met with constant disappointment, frustration, and ultimately more anger. Instead of feeling the need to protect the one who dumped the eggs as she originally did, she begins to outwardly express her anger toward him. She's constantly being hit with new problems she has neither encountered to date, nor anticipated. She finds herself taking mental timeouts and grasping for visualizations to give herself strength. This woman is very tired.

What I know now:

- You'll feel sorry for yourself. It's ok. You've been handed a huge mess to deal with. Wallow for a while if you need to and it makes you feel better.
- You might continue to feel angrier and angrier, even about little things.

61

- It's normal to find yourself filling the deceased person's role in your life with others.
- Visualization and mind games can make you feel stronger.
- Scheduling things you used to do with friends provides nice moments of normalcy.
- Journaling is a fantastic way to release anxiety. I've never been one to keep diaries or journals, but mine became a life line for me.
- Take comfort in the fact the deceased had no idea of the far-reaching impact this would have on your life. It might feel like it was directed at you, it wasn't. No one could foresee every nuance of what you're going through.
- If you don't have to tell credit card companies, utility companies, banks, etc. he's gone, don't. At least not for now.
- If you know it's going to be necessary to tell someone, take a friend with you, or ask them to help you with the phone call, in case you have trouble with the conversation.
- Do everything on your own timeline, not others. Things such as opening sympathy cards, deciding what to do with your loved one's belongings...
- Be ok with not living exactly as societal norms would dictate. Just do what makes you the most comfortable. It's ok!

April 18, 2015

During his initial visit to my house, the leader of the SOS group mentioned that in the weeks after his son died, there were several occasions he abandoned a full cart of groceries in the middle of an aisle and walked out. I had one of those grocery moments today, for a different reason than he did. It wasn't very pretty but I managed to make it to the car with my groceries before completely breaking down.

The reason for the breakdown probably seems very petty to some. Everything seemed so expensive. I felt I had to buy different things than I normally do. The cheapest of everything…milk, tomatoes, apples. With the security of two incomes, it never crossed my mind. It just felt like one more pile of shit he threw in my face by doing what he did. What a fucker to leave me here to fend for myself. Didn't it occur to him my entire lifestyle was based around two salaries, not one? Didn't it occur to him that all of a sudden, I'd have to buy the cheap crap instead of what I'm used to. Or that I would have to cook at home instead of eating out like I'm used to? Even when we ate at home, he cooked. I hate cooking and I'm not even good at it. Second rate cooking with second rate ingredients. Sounds appetizing.

I understand my grocery problem is not tragic by any means, but it's yet one more unexpected, sudden change to my life. A life that's really not going so well at the moment. Another change I didn't ask for. One that was completely senseless and avoidable. It's not like he got hit by a train, the asshole actually chose to leave me in this situation. What a great guy. Well who knows, I suppose it's possible he would have been hit by a train on that day anyway, but at least he wouldn't have made a choice to screw up my life. It would still suck but the train scenario would have been easier to accept.

Poor Mike had to deal with me coming into the house sobbing, with my four tiny bags of groceries which seemed to cost a million dollars. He had a really nice day going too, so I'm sorry to put him through my meltdown. I didn't tell him the problem because I don't want him to feel obligated to pay for anything right now. Or worry about it.

Another poop pile I had to deal with today was working through some more bills I didn't understand. Mike was out golfing. I had a crying fit, cursing Scott out loud for leaving me with all of this. He knew I hated paperwork. He knew I'd have to do all of it from now on. And…he left anyway. Like I was supposed to magically know how to do something he's done for literally 25 years? Right. Of course, it couldn't be simple. There's the personal crap, the business crap, the other business crap, and the mystery crap that doesn't seem to fit anywhere. It's hard to even know where to start. But I did manage to make some progress today with Mike's help. I have a call in to the insurance agent and hope to meet with the banker and the accountant next week. I'd like to say I have a sense of accomplishment, or pride I'm figuring it out…but really, I just feel bitter that I have to do it.

Something really cool happened last night right before bed. Kim texted me a picture of an antler an animal shed in her driveway. Her comment said, "I found this buried in the snow in my driveway this morning. Kinda nasty, kinda neat." It was exactly three weeks from the day Scott did it. He was supposed to be up in the hills hiking around with friends, looking for shed antlers on the day he died. WOW. Kim said Scott found a way to leave a "treat" for me. He always brought me pretty rocks and other items from nature he found when he was out in the woods. I hope she's right. I hope he's happy wherever he is. But I'm still so angry with him it's hard to have much concern for his well-being right now. I'm so desperately hoping I see him again someday, but the anger I feel towards him is a huge conflict with my hope for his happiness.

April 19, 2015

Much better day than yesterday but still a stinker at times. Opening Scott's closet to look for hangars was a mistake. When I saw his clothes hanging there, the only thing I could think is his body is no longer here to wear everything I loved seeing him wear. A very sad and difficult moment. I cried about it for a while, then moved on with the day.

Mike and I attended a different church this morning then met my friends, Sam and Sarah, for coffee. We met ten years ago or so when Scott and I attended the same church as they do. At the service I was still feeling very down about the closet incident and didn't feel like talking. When Sarah tried to make a few comments during the service, I pretty much ignored her. In the past, I would have felt rude ignoring someone, but right now I don't. I know Sarah didn't take it that way.

Just like the bad moments are so unpredictable, so are the moments that seem to provide just what I need, at just the right time. I sat there thinking, not paying much attention to the sermon. There was one thing though I heard and gained strength from. The daily handout was very colorful and pretty and said "Walk Strong" on the front of it. During the sermon, I tuned in just in time to hear the pastor say, God wants us to be like solid trees with our roots firmly planted in Christ. Something about this statement made me feel stronger. Next time we stood up and for the rest of the day, I've pictured myself as a big, tall, strong, sturdy tree. My feet confidently planted on the new ground I'm walking on. Sturdy Tree. Walk Strong. It made a difference.

Coffee with Sam and Sarah was relaxing. Mike hit it off with Sam and they discussed golfing together in the future. We talked about Sam's desire to get a part time job, and types of jobs that might work for him. He's 80, takes a lot of drugs as a result of many surgeries, and is worried about passing a drug test. We talked about normal things normal people talk about, under normal circumstances. It was actually a fun, light, moment in which I almost felt…well, normal.

My dad, who lives about two-hours away by car sent Mike a text that said: "the silence up there is deafening, what did you do today?" I've only spoken to my parents twice since this happened. I haven't seen my dad. He wasn't able to attend the funeral. I'm worried about spending time with them right now because I don't want them to sense the distress that's become such a big part of my daily life. Of course, they know it's there. I'm just worried letting them actually witness it with their own eyes and ears would make it too real for them. I don't want them to worry about me. I'm not sure how to act around them, happy, sad, in-between? I definitely can't let them see one of my fall-apart moments. Maybe I'm wrong and making problems where none exist. Karen suggested just trying to text more for now to at least keep them involved. I'll do that. They invited Mike and I to visit next weekend to eat crawfish. This is something we did in the past…except Scott was there.

April 20, 2015

It's 2:00 am. I often wake up in the middle of the night and can't go back to sleep because my mind is going a million miles an hour. It usually gets stuck on one thought. Different ones, but they all get stuck. Over and over and over. Two things sometimes help. Writing down whatever is going around in my brain is the first. The second is breaking up the stuck thought process by focusing on other things, things that aren't concerning or threatening in any way. Surfing the internet, watching TV… Reading doesn't work because it requires concentration which seems to be completely absent these days.

This time a dream woke me. I've been having generally bad/disturbing dreams...accidentally running over my sister with a car, something bad about my dad I can't remember, etc. Just dreams that make me wake up feeling crappy. Rarely about Scott. I've only had two dreams about him since he died. In both of them he was comforting and encouraging me. I guess my sleep brain isn't as angry with him as my awake brain.

This time I was dreaming I was supposed to make a speech introducing Neil's daughter and her husband at some unknown ceremony. On the drive to the ceremony, with several of his immediate family members, I realized my notes didn't make any sense. Some of the information was wrong, and I had drawn a bunch of pictures that didn't make any sense. In my speech I was going to talk about them being a "couple of contrast." I planned to talk about how they were similar, and how they were different. And how they fit together perfectly in this study of contrast. I kept obsessing about the pictures I'd drawn and what they meant. On the drive I was handing out Bounce sheets to everyone in the car. I told them it would help to calm their nerves. When we got to the site of the ceremony, it was a church. I asked Neil for a printer, so I could modify the speech which was to happen in thirty minutes. The church had no printer. I had to scribble in the margins but as I started doing so, I worried about those pictures. I couldn't make a whole story from them that made any sense. I had thought I would be able to. I was panicking because I didn't know how I was supposed to get up in front of a crowd and talk about two people I knew nothing about.

Earlier in the dream, several women who were attending the ceremony came to my house to get me. I had a goldfish in a bowl. But the bowl was so dirty you couldn't even see the fish swimming around. My sister was trying to help me clean it. I thought, I can't even take care of a little goldfish.

Same day but much later... The instructors are still tentative around me. I wonder if they wonder why I'm still wearing my wedding ring. Or why I'm wearing Scott's watch. One of them stopped by my office on his way home to say, "I just wanted to tell you it's good to have you back." If Doug hadn't been sitting there, I would have started crying.

Made it through the day with only one crying jag. I had to call a dentist to schedule an appointment...and ask if I could get in before the end of the month. Asking people for things, or having to explain things that include the phrase, "my husband passed away," is a conversation I can't have without breaking down. In this case, I needed my appointment before the end of the month because I'm not sure if my new COBRA insurance will cover it when Scott's expires. I don't even know what COBRA is but for some reason, admitting to people I have it feels shameful.

Before I left work tonight, I sat and talked to Neil for two hours about the bible, how to study it, and how to know which pastors are biblically sound. I sent Pastor Craig a text a couple of days ago asking for a confidential meeting. He's the pastor who was at my house that day. He also performed Scott's service. His response was he and his wife would be honored to meet with me. Seemed weird. I asked for a confidential meeting and he invited her. I told Neil about my request and Craig's response. He said because there's so much hanky-panky between pastors and church members these days, Craig is ultra-careful to avoid any appearance of wrong-doing. Neil also said Craig would do the same with his wife, Jennifer, if she asked him for a meeting. All of this led to the two-hour discussion of the bible.

I was supposed to meet Amy for lunch today, but she texted me she was sick. It felt like a crushing blow. I was looking forward to seeing her. It felt important to stick to my plan, so I texted Mike asking him if wanted to meet. He said yes, so I said I'd text him "around 12:30" when I was ready to leave my office. That way he could leave the house at the same time. When I sent him a text at 12:35 saying I could head over, he was already there. In and Out Burger. This upset me. Scott and I would meet for lunch commonly and, over the years, had learned to understand each other's timing. My brother and I don't have the same timing, one more reminder of the intricate pieces of a relationship now non-existent. Mike isn't a replacement for Scott, but he's filling a hole while I ease into my new life. It wasn't Mike I was mad at, it was the shit situation. I doubt if he thought about it that deeply. He just had to hear me being mad again.

April 21, 2015

I made it through my shower this morning without crying. Twice in five days, a new record. Someone call Guinness. I did a Robert Downey Jr. thing. I imagined myself stepping onto the elevated, round platform he steps onto in the Ironman movies…just before all those the robot arms snap his suit of armor into place. My platform was actually a tiny drain hole. I stood over it, not on it. Put my arms down, extended my fingers, chin up, then imagined my suit of armor was God surrounding me for the day. I

70

imagined I was a solid tree with feet planted firmly on the ground to withstand whatever the day threw at me. First, I thought I'd be an oak tree. Then I upgraded to a giant redwood.

On the way to meet with Jill, Joel Osteen (JO as I've begun calling him), said, "He rewards people who seek after him." I texted it to Neil...dang it, driving and texting again, determined to stop that...and asked, "Is this an incorrect statement?" He said the statement is "absolutely correct" and gave me two bible scriptures to read, Hebrews 11:6: "But without faith it is impossible to please Him, for he who comes to God must believe that He is, and that He is a rewarder of those who diligently seek Him." And Revelation 3:20. Have not read that one yet...

I was feeling composed when I sat down in Jill's office. Two minutes later... not so much. Which was ironic since on the drive over, I felt pretty good and thought to myself, I hope she doesn't think I'm not grieving properly because I'm not all weepy like her other clients. Nope, no worries there.

I sometimes send Jill my journal for the week, so she asked about the goldfish dream. I feel like I failed Scott. We talked about mindsets of those who do this and how it's not about me or anyone around him, it's about him. We can't keep questioning the "what ifs." There is no answer. It's not about any of those things. It's about him. I can't control what he did any more than someone could control another person's anxiety attack or bout of depression. She said this...I listened. But I still wonder if I had been kinder, more understanding, more compassionate that morning, would this have happened. Maybe there will come a day I can accept her perfectly rational logic. This is not the day.

My emotions are far stronger than my logic right now. Far stronger. As in, not even in the ballpark stronger. It's a very strange, and very uncomfortable place for me to be. On the drive home, JO said "It's not the end, it's a new beginning."

The dentist visit was difficult too. "Is anything bothering you?" was the question of the day posted on the waiting room wall. Nope, all good. Just here for a cleaning and regular checkup. Oh, and by the way, my husband of nearly 24 years shot himself less than a month ago. And yes please to the cinnamon flavored polish. Ended up leaving in tears after the lady who squeezed me into the schedule came out and introduced herself to me. I left without getting my teeth cleaned.

On the drive back to work JO was speaking to men about how marriage is a commitment, and how they're meant to take care of their wives. You hear that, I said out loud? A commitment. You were supposed to take care of me. Nice job. I kept the commitment, you didn't. And I certainly don't feel taken care of.

Crying has become a bodily function like eating and peeing. When I get hungry I eat, full bladder I find a bathroom. When I start to cry, I just do. Deal with the wash of emotion, feel it and then move on. This too shall pass. Famous quote I think.

Spoke with Scott's brother, "RichardSorryPeter" (RSP) tonight. His name was Richard, he changed it to Peter a couple of years ago, I can never get it right and that's what I always end up calling him. After talking with Jill about my situation and returning to work gradually, I wondered if RSP had the same luxury. Does he have to put on a happy face? Or does he have the space to allow his process to run its course.

I've heard the best way to help yourself is to help others. When he called, he sounded very down. It was empowering for me to be the one saying, "You'll be ok. You can do this." All his clients know his situation and have been a good support system for him. He's also had the "awkwards", those who don't quite know what to say. I reminded him they're doing the best they can. It's a sucko situation for everyone. No one really knows what to say or do. "Let me know if I can help" is a perfect example of a well-intended but very misguided statement in this situation. If would be easier if they would just think of something and do it.

RSP doesn't have a group, or even an individual counselor. He's going to look for resources. I'm going to try to find someone in the local groups who's lost a brother and would talk to him on the phone. He and I are in this mess together, but another male who lost a brother would be a closer match for him than I am. RSP and I discussed our mutual desire to move through this and come out joyful on the other side. We don't want to become those group members who seem to enjoy wallowing in misery especially with other members who will be their wallow buddies.

He asked me if I have a "time line." He meant for dealing with the grief. Oddly enough, just this morning I was thinking about exactly that. I decided one year and one month is enough. A year to get through of the "firsts" everyone says are difficult, and a month to get past the anniversary of the worst month of my life. The extra month is a little cushion. A little wiggle room. JO says the front window of a car is much bigger than the rearview mirror because it's what's ahead of us that counts, not what's already behind us. He's a smart cracker.

Even Ironman doesn't sleep in his armor. Day Armor off. Night Armor on. I haven't gotten the Night Armor dialed in yet...probably something fuzzy, soft, big and floppy covering me from head to toe with just a little breathing hole by my nose. The color will change from night to night I think. Depending on my mood. Tonight, green feels right.

April 22, 2015

Every day it's something else. Something completely unexpected and unpredictable. Today, I don't even know what "it" was. The day had been a bit melancholy, then out of the blue it struck me again. He's not coming back. I'm in this on my own now. Maybe it was running around this morning doing things he normally did...putting gas in my car, shoveling dirt back into the same hole the dogs dug for the umpteenth time, feeding the pets, emptying the dishwasher before work, stopping at the bank to pick up paper work, opening the mail. It's not that I never did any of these things, I've just never been responsible for all of them, all the time. It's overwhelming for me, and I'm even a very organized person. When is there time to move forward with anything when all I do is stomp out the immediate fires? New life: Fire. Stomp. Fire. Stomp. Repeat.

Vicki came to visit. I asked for her help opening the sympathy cards I've been avoiding. It's pretty awful reading how much he meant to all these people and their fur kids. And all the picture of the lovely pets he left behind. I was most sad for them because he's no longer here to care for them. He left them too. Vicki told me that at the funeral, a woman said her young daughter had come to see Scott as a father figure after her own father passed away. Nice work Scott, on top of all the other destruction you caused, there's that. A sad little girl. We got through about half the cards then pushed the pause button. To be resumed another day. I should feel happy he touched so many lives…but really, I just feel angry he took himself out of those lives. So many of them.

A box arrived from Colorado. I imagine it's the antlers Kim found in her driveway. As she put it, the "treat" he left for me. Probably won't be able to open it for quite a while, and I texted her as much. She wrote back "you do what you can do and nothing else. When you're ready, you'll know." Kim always knows the right thing to say. She lost her mother rather suddenly last year. It was on my birthday.

April 23, 2015

SOS Group was weird tonight. After weeks of good and bad waves, I was in a good wave. I had been warned to expect them. The drive over with Jennifer and Jen was fun, and light. As we drove into the parking lot, we saw two pair of geese and their babies, all hanging out as a group. Just being cute. Sitting in group on a good wave, still happy in my head about the little baby geese, but feeling really exhausted from the long day, I emotionally checked out. I had very little interest in, or empathy for, what others had to say. Just kind of a "Hmmm, that's nice" attitude.

My thoughts wandered everywhere...I counted the people in the group, calculated how long we were going to be there. Wondered why everyone had a bottle of water except me? How long has it been since I washed the shorts I'm wearing? They look grubby. Probably been awhile considering in the couple of weeks after he did it I wore pretty much the same thing every day. Is that a Rolex that guy is wearing? Nope, knock off. Could I check my phone without being noticed? Don't care, checked it, one message. Why are we listening to someone go on and on about how "aggravated" he is because the new drummer in his band has a bad attitude and because "my guitarist is a drunk." Really? That's how awful your life is? Is it just me or does that sound a bit petty in a room full of people who've lost someone to suicide? Dude, reality check. Right now, I find very little in life to be aggravating. Big "problems" and "concerns" from before have become tiny little specks in my world.

The leader said it's ok to be angry. It can even be a good thing for a while. The last 30 seconds of someone's life does not define the person. In Scott's case there were 49 other years. He was so young. It doesn't seem real when I see the number in writing. 49. He also said, when someone makes the decision to do it, they're at peace and can take care of business before doing it. Scott did. He bought dog food and sent out a business email. Had he made the decision at that time? The why's and what if's will never be known and, per the group, eventually need to stop being a part of my thought process. Because there are no answers for most people. Besides, it doesn't change anything…the end result is the same.

Yes, weird group tonight. I think my brain said enough for now then switched the channel to a more pleasant station. No doubt, the waves will come again when the heart and emotions overrule the brain.

April 24, 2015

"This is what I most closely correlate to a shit storm and cluster eff all wrapped up into a healthy serving of WTF!!!" That was a text from Floyd, his summary of what Scott created when he made his decision. Floyd and his wife Anne were our friends, now I guess they're just mine. He says he can't wrap his head around what happened. Today pretty much felt like Floyd's assessment. Times ten. So much for my tough guy attitude in group yesterday.

It got off to a bad start when I didn't get much sleep last night after getting home late from group. Going back to sleep once I wake up is impossible. It's the jumble of awful thoughts preventing me from going back to sleep. As a result, I was already exhausted when I got to work. It went downhill from there.

I called the bank holding my car lease to figure out final payments and payoff cost should I decide to go that route. Having to explain why it's me calling, not the "primary" on the account, is always way beyond my ability at this time. The tears flow, the person on the other end of the line is uncomfortable, and sometimes says they're sorry to hear about my situation. About an hour after arriving at work, I left. Snuck out the back and drove to a local park to walk around. I paid attention to birds, clouds, everything... hoping for a sign from Scott.

From the park, I went home to clean up. The accountant asked me to call the credit card company to give permission for him to have read-only access to the accounts. Long story short, the credit card thieves cancelled ALL my credit cards because the "primary" on the account is deceased. Two businesses and a personal account. All of them. Closed. I'm completely credit card-less. Then to add insult to injury, they cheerfully offered me the opportunity to apply for my own cards. Denied. I would receive an explanation in the mail in five business days. What? My credit score is higher than Scott's. As Floyd said, W.T.F.

I called Neil in hysterics to tell him what happened. After I explained he said, "Is that it?" What do you mean "is that it?" He said, "It's not a big deal, I thought someone was in an accident or something." It's a big deal to me. He said to use my work credit card until Monday when he'll take me to the bank to get a new card.

Earl the accountant was so sweet. When I called him, he was dumb-founded. "If they knew who you were they would send a car to pick you up and help you apply for the card." Always sweet Earl. A little dramatic. He's kind, smart, thoughtful, and Scott trusted him. So, I do too. He said he could get me new cards tomorrow if I want his help. Told him Neil and I had a plan, but thanks.

Frustration seems to bubble over so easily at pretty much anything. So yeah, I had a very crappy day after such a peaceful evening the night before. Sometimes I just feel blasted from every angle at the same time. Constantly being reminded he is no longer here to help with anything. Or to just to sit quietly with on the couch. Seems to be no time to sit quietly on the couch anyway, there's always more to do. More paperwork, more to clean, more to cook, furry mouths to feed or walk, and it goes on and on and on. Even if I could sleep, I wonder if there would even be time for that. Scott you pig. Even an evening walk with Diane didn't lift the cloud enveloping me today. Week four, complete.

Therapist's reflections:

So much comes into question when dealing with a loss to suicide. Nothing is as you thought it was previously. Nothing! Although you've been completely aware of this trauma since the day your loved one died, your mind has protected you with shock and denial. One thing has remained unwavering - the question of WHY? Why did they do this? Why did they choose to leave me, our family? Why didn't they reach out for help?

Through my many years of practice and experience in suicide loss, I've come to believe, in most cases, the act of suicide is an irrational, three to five-minute act. A person can be depressed, or even actively contemplating suicide, yet live. For some; however, there is a perfect storm of events which causes those in intense psychological pain to become so irrational they believe the world will always be as dark as it is in that moment. In that desperate moment, those who are suicidal believe their loved ones are better off without them. They believe they are a burden to those around them. In this irrational mindset, someone who is suicidal often thinks they are doing us a favor. Remember, if you have a healthy and rational mind, you cannot understand an unhealthy and irrational thought process. It's not possible. Your search for WHY may never really provide you any clarity. My clients tell me they just wake up one day and stop asking.

Anger is also a natural part of this process and often times, is uncomfortable to acknowledge. There is guilt associated with being angry with our loved ones. "How can I be mad at them if they were in so much pain they felt they needed to end their lives?" Again, do not try to rationalize an irrational act.

Anger is important to grief. Your loved one let you down. They left you alone. Because of suicide, your life is currently in complete disarray. Even if you aren't mad at your loved one, you have every right to be angry with the situation. You can be angry that you now have to re-write your future; you have to deal with all the financial ramifications; you have to answer people's questions about your family dynamics, which have drastically changed. You can be angry at mental illness, if it was a part of your loved one's demise. You can be angry without laying blame. Because we know there's no one person, or thing, responsible for another person's life. Many times, I've said, "I don't worry most about those who are angry. I worry most about those who don't get angry." It's an important part of the grief process.

What I noticed in Missy during this time:

Missy felt abandoned, betrayed, and deserted during this time. She felt bogged down with daily chores - chores normally handled by Scott. She was overwhelmed with the financial aspect of losing a spouse to suicide, and all the hoops necessary to jump through. Each hoop involved telling her story all over again. This was painful for Missy.

Missy would attend group meetings, read books, and declare she wasn't going to be one of "those" Survivors. She wasn't going to be in deep grief years from now. She was resolute she would process differently, more efficiently. She believed she was more resilient than other Survivors. I just smiled.

Chapter 6

The Fifth Week

*As long as one
keeps searching,
the answers come.*

Joan Baez

Looking back:

The woman has come to understand the broken eggs cannot be repaired and even the basket they were in can't be salvaged. Although accepting this fact is frightening enough to her, it's the actual process of cleaning up the mess that's beginning to take a toll on this woman. Despite being physically, mentally, and emotionally exhausted, she's not slowing down. Busyness is her safe zone. Physically she's not taking care of herself, her mental abilities are in decline, and her unpredictable emotions are surprising her.

In her exhaustion, it's as though someone has removed the earmuffs she's been wearing since the day the eggs were dumped. Everything seems loud and exaggerated. Simultaneously though, parts of her that have been absent, for what feels like an eternity, are waking up. Parts that have served her well in the past such as her sense of humor, her sarcastic wit, and her resolve to succeed.

What I know now:

- You've made it through an entire month. Awesome job, this is an amazing accomplishment. Keep going!
- The back and forth between grief and relief is unbelievably difficult. It might feel like it's never going to end. It will.
- Angry starts to feel angrier, sad starts to feel sadder, happy starts to feel happier. Your brain is waking up from the complete shock and numbness it's been living in.
- Are you angry at the person who did this? I was furious.
- Sometimes you feel like this is your life now…and you hate it. It is for now but know something for sure…it's not your life forever, you will move through this.
- If it hasn't already happened, you will eventually gain enough strength to begin purposely healing and making your life right again.
- You might feel like you can't remember anything.
- Little things will be blessings to you, grab onto them and appreciate.

April 25, 2015 - 4:00 am.

It feels like when Scott did what he did he sentenced me to a life of sadness, anger, frustration, and general misery. This is pretty much the feeling for the morning as well as all day yesterday. Like I just can't escape it no matter what I do or what people say. Waking up early is horrible. My mind immediately goes into overdrive and feels like a herd of wild horses racing toward a cliff. There are no good thoughts that come from lying in bed for hours as I try hopelessly to go back to sleep. Unfortunately, this has become a routine. I've not had the experience others talk about when they wake up and forget what has happened. Then the realization strikes them. I remember the very instant I wake up.

Today is the big day to see my dad for the first time and my mom for the second. The first was at the service. Maybe the anticipation is what has caused the recent funk? I haven't taken any of the day-medication since the first week but took one today before we left. Mike is driving, I'm typing. I told Karen how I was feeling about the life sentence and she said, "I know it sucks and hurts right now. However, as I've said many times before, you are the only one who can allow yourself to be sentenced to a life of misery. You must go through this pain to get to the other side. But, it will be your choice alone in your decision to move forward."

Other "survivors" have mentioned the build up to any of the big events is worse than the actual day itself. They were right, at least for today. But the constant roller coaster, OMG! Up and down and up and down…more of the same. I'm beginning to worry during the good times now because it has always meant the cliff is just around the corner. I guess a better approach would be to accept the good and when the little choo choo falls off the track again, pick it up and give it another push.

April 26, 2015

My first ever, and most likely last ever Facebook post. Actually, "post" is giving myself too much credit, I sent a letter to the manager at Scott's clinic and asked her to do it for me.

Dear Crossroads Clients and Staff,

I don't know how to begin to thank you all for your kindness in this period of terrible and overwhelming sadness. Without the word of God, dear friends and family, and those of you who knew him through the clinic who have reached out to me, I could not have made it this far. Your cards, visits, phone calls, attendance at the service, offers to help, etc. have been a complete blessing in this difficult time and I wish I could thank each of you personally. I have yet to finish reading all of the cards as I can only manage a handful at a time. Your words are emotional, and the pictures of your beautiful babies are so lovely and so heart wrenching all at the same time.

Scott loved each and every client and co-worker and beautiful little critter he was so privileged to care for. I realized that not only do I mourn his absence I also mourn the loss of the stories he would tell me about you all. He truly loved his job and the people with whom he got to spend his days. We always laughed that it was impossible to go anywhere without running into someone who knew him. If I had a dime for every time I heard "I LOVE your husband!" He would apologize for not making introductions after you walked away, saying he couldn't recall people names sometimes but he always remembered the pet names. For someone that could be as forgetful as he could be he was amazing at remembering the names of your pets.

For everything you saw of him in his capacity as your vet or co-worker, he was more at home. Loving, caring, thoughtful, smart, creative, non-judgmental, funny, silly, hardworking...he was all that and so much more. He has been my best friend since we met 27 years ago and definitely the best part of me. The saying about someone being your better half does not even begin to apply here. He was my better 9/10's and I miss that part of me so much, for so many reasons, and in so many ways. He wasn't perfect, but he was perfect for me.

Like I said, there are no words to thank everyone adequately, but please know how much of a difference your support has made. I also know it means the world to Scott. I hope that someday I have a chance to make a difference in someone's life the way that you all have made a difference in mine. I do not have much to offer but if I can do any little tiny thing for anyone, please do not hesitate to reach out and ask. I will be there for you.

Sincerely,
Missy Palrang

April 27, 2015

Yesterday at Costco, someone referred to my brother as my husband. It was a bitter pill to swallow but I just smiled and said, "He's my brother, not my husband." No further explanation. I was glad he had walked away and didn't hear it, not sure why but it would have made it worse for me if he had.

Two nights in a row of waking in the middle of the night and being unable to go back to sleep. My brain churns and churns and won't let up. After about an hour I got up to try to read something. Pointless. No concentration to remember anything. So, novels are out. Baby came and lay on my chest and purred. It was so relaxing I decided to see if I can find a CD with just a purring cat. Maybe that would help.

The day was busy. Went to the bank to get credit cards…fortunately Neil went with me because as usual, it was impossible to get through the meeting. The banker is working on new cards for me.

Scott's cousin Aliza is in town to meet with the wives of local Rabbis and discuss their place in the community. Fascinating woman! She's a year older than me and moved to Israel when she was 16 and converted to Judaism. Now she teaches and has a wonderfully caring spirit. She lost a 19-year-old son to suicide just under 2 years ago. She suggested "scheduling grief" …designating a time to allow the grief to flow. Interesting. I don't know if it would work for me or not. It did for her. So many words of wisdom to be lost in my fuzzy brain. Not a lot is sticking at the moment…I need to start carrying around a notebook for these meetings.

Dinner with Randy's family. His 12-year-old son said the prayer before dinner and included "Please help Miss Missy to feel better." It choked me up to hear him say this, but I didn't want to be a crier at the table. I held it in. What a special gift he gave me. Randy later told me they've been saying it every night. While small blessings in this sickening situation don't change it, they provide small, but temporary reprieves. I'll take any small reprieve right now.

I worry that constantly making myself busy is distracting from the process of healing that needs to begin. Or continue. Maybe it's already happening. Not sure where I am in the spectrum.

April 28, 2015

When I couldn't sleep again I turned on my phone and computer to find something to do. They both said the time was 3:26. Of course they did. The numbers 326 and 327 have been appearing in my life for years. I've always noticed them. Scott was born on 3/26. He died on 3/27.

I feel completely shattered on the inside and like my skin on the outside is beginning to fall apart as well. Like it's no longer able to hold the inside pieces together. You can't glue a glass together once it's been smashed on the sidewalk. You can't even find all the pieces. What you do find is just dust, destroyed forever. Dreams are getting worse. Since I'm awake much of the night I can't remember which things happened when I was awake, and which were in a dream.

Yesterday I asked Randy what he thought about talking to someone who says he communicates with the dead. Someone approached me a couple of weeks ago with the idea. Neil told me earlier not to. He said, "Please please please please do not consider doing this." Randy said he thought it would be ok. They are the two most biblically sound people I know, who is right?

In my dream this time, Randy and his wife Rachele, were taking care of me, keeping an eye on me 24 hours a day, even taking me to work with them. Rachele brought a man to the house who could speak with the dead. I wasn't sure I wanted to talk to him. In the dream the man was impatient, he had places to go and was doing Randy and Rachele a favor by being there to help me. I couldn't decide if I wanted to do it or not.

Right before bed I spoke with Jan. She had two years of lawsuits to manage after her husband died seven years ago. When they were over she "crashed." Am I crashing? No lawsuits to resolve but the service is over. I'm staying way busier than I like. She said to get back to my exercise routine. I've been walking much more than before. Sitting at home with nothing to do is hard. Can't concentrate to read a book, have lost all interest in TV, so I just busy myself. Is that avoidance of grieving? Should I be doing it differently? My calendar is booked for the next couple of weeks. Lunch dates, appointments. Evenings too. It's too much, I'm not a social person.

Obviously lack of sleep is not helping. Medication again last night. I had gone with just melatonin last couple of nights. Tonight was a low dose, half pill, of the sleeping pills I've been given. Maybe it was not enough because here I am in the middle of the night again. Everyone says how important sleep is but it isn't coming. When it does, it's dark and disturbing. Always dark, at night, or in a dark room.

Maybe I'm just crashing because Jan did. Maybe she suggested it and I heard it. Maybe if I hadn't heard her experience I wouldn't be doing this. It took her about a year after the crash to feel ok. She said something called "EMDR" worked wonders for her. I just want to scream. I'm so angry. He has turned me into, everything I don't want to be, but there is no fix for this. Nothing people can say or do makes a difference.

April 29, 2015

I caved and took the larger dose of the sleeping pill and actually got a decent night sleep - around seven hours with no nightmares. I guess it's ok for now? The day was not bad perhaps because of the sleep or perhaps because I'm on the upswing from the latest crash. It's sad that good days lead me to worry about the bad ones inevitably around the corner.

I was hoping today was "the day," the one to make it through without crying. Nope. Unbroken string of days intact. The plan for July was Scott, Karen, my mom, and myself would go on a cruise to Greece. Tickets booked, ready to go. One more up-yours delivered by Scott's actions. The airlines are absolutely unbending on allowing me to pass his ticket on to someone else. As if they'll suffer because someone besides Scott would be occupying the seat next to me. Wow, what a tragedy it would be for them. Obviously some critical, red alert situation the rest of us aren't privy to. Who knows what a little compassion and understanding on their part might lead to. Long story short, most likely we are all going to cancel. Sounds like I can get my money back, Karen and mom will have to take a credit requiring a fee to rebook. Thieves.

Funny situation today. One of our students recently did poorly on an oral and flight test. According to the check instructor, when he didn't know a few answers, he resigned and got a whipped puppy attitude. I happen to like this kid and see potential in him. He's not terribly skilled or smart, but he has desire and is a hard worker. I called him into my office and talked to him about not giving up and when you do that in a helicopter, you're going to hurt or kill people. "Never give up. Life will throw you difficult situations, but you have to keep trying. Even if you do something wrong, do it with confidence and don't quit." My speech was something like this, except much more long winded. About halfway through, it occurred to me I was talking to myself as much as I was to him. Never give up.

Jodi from Farmers Insurance was kind enough to stop by to help me organize and plan for insurance payments. First, I had to learn WHAT I have insured, then there was the sticker shock of learning how much it costs to have all the crap insured. Jodi has to change everything to my name only and will come back with folders of everything organized. People have been so kind and giving. I mean, an insurance agent who takes her time, after hours, to come to my house? Then set up a filing system for me? I'm a good judge of people. She's a good one.

April 30, 2015

Still didn't achieve "the day." Cried several times about the little things. I'm trying to find a counselor who will do EMDR therapy, but it's become an exercise in frustration. Everyone is either booked until August, or doesn't accept insurance…not just my insurance, any insurance. Weekly visits would cost six to eight hundred dollars a month. I couldn't do that.

Scott's family in Oregon has decided to have not just one more get together to remember him, but two. One in May and one in August. Neil helped me formulate a plan to let them know I don't wish to attend. The truth is, going to these memorials would feel like going backwards. The service and reception we already did were perfect. I believe Scott would have liked them. My job is to move forward now. But it's hard, every day is emotionally draining, sad, unpredictable and sometimes feels impossible to get through. But at least time is passing. I see it like I'm sitting in a boat drifting down a 1000-mile stream. The current will get me there when it gets me there. I can lay in the bottom of the boat like a lump, smashing into rocks, scraping under overhanging tree branches, and getting stuck in eddies going around and around for days. Or I can grab the oars and figure out how to navigate around the obstacles. Regardless of the approach taken, the destination will be the same but the person in the boat at the end of the journey will not. I have to be the captain of my boat.

May 1, 2015

I seem to be the Queen of Analogies lately. Last night, walking with Di, we saw Vicki in her front yard and stopped to talk. She was battling her sprinkler system. A couple of weeks ago she noticed a bush which is supposed to be light green, was actually two toned. Light green and dark green. Her lawn man dug around in the bush and found a gigantic weed grown into the bush. It had been trimmed right along with the bush the last few times it was trimmed. Weird. He removed the weed which left the poor bush looking scraggly, like half of it was missing. Lying in bed this morning it occurred to me my life feels like the bush. Half of me is missing. I guess the good news is, like the bush, with the proper care I can grow into those holes to be a full bush again.

Another queen moment was the analogy I had regarding my reasons for not wanting to attend memorials number two and three planned for Scott. It's a pilot thing. I'm imagining I'm flying on a heading of 360 (North)…I can turn as far left as 270 (West) or as far right at 090 (East) without going backwards. Moving forward doesn't have to mean moving in a straight line, it can mean wandering all over the sky as long as I don't turn beyond those headings. 269 or 091 would be, even though just by one degree, a backward trajectory. It's ok to wander around trying to navigate this new course. Going to services two and/or three would, in my head mean flying outside of my approved course, the one taking me forward. It's probably not a great plan to explain it to Scott's family in those terms.

Still exactly zero cry-free days. I can't even remember what caused it today. I just remember looking at the clock at 10:00 am when the tears started, and thinking, well at least I made it until ten today. Overall though, the day was calm. I've had several in a row now. Is the cliff looming? I really hope it's not, but I'm not optimistic based on history so far.

Today's dose of JO taught the importance of setting, writing down, and striving towards goals. If you don't set a goal, you certainly won't achieve it. Success and progress are not accidental. He says to set goals both short and long term. My short-term goal: make it through a day without crying. Not just because I'm sucking it up. Because I really don't feel the need to cry. Seems simple. Long-term goals: I have some in my head but don't want to write them down. If I don't achieve them, I won't feel like a failure. It seems less failure-ish if the goal was only in my head anyway.

FINALLY, I found a therapist who will do EMDR with me. OMGosh who would have thought it would be this difficult. Even this one can't meet weekly, but at this point I'll accept what she can do - every other week. We begin on the 13th of May.

Maybe this is a good thing but I'm not feeling as much of a need/desire to write all the time. I'm starting to bore myself. Since I'm the intended audience, that's pretty bad.

Therapist's reflections:

We've heard the phrase "she's going into shock," or "he's obviously in shock" associated with a trauma or event that's difficult to process. Often, the cause is an accident, intense physical pain, or even a highly emotional experience. The person experiencing shock may turn pale, become dizzy, begin sweating, feel nauseous, and disconnect mentally. Left untreated, shock can cause permanent organ failure or even death.

But what happens when we come out of shock? No one ever tells us what that's like. Missy referenced it in this chapter when she said, "Everything seems loud and exaggerated." I call this phase of suicide grief the Punch to the Gut.

Imagine yourself as a medieval Knight. You are suited with armor made of plated steel and chain mail. As a Survivor, shock and denial provide this armor for you. It protects you from the looks of disbelief, the judgmental words, and the reality your loved one is never returning.

As these first weeks of grief pass into months, the shock and denial begin to fade away. As they leave, they slowly take an article of your protective armor with them. It's my experience in working with hundreds of families that this phase occurs roughly six to eight weeks from when the loss occurred. The Punch to the Gut leaves you feeling vulnerable without your protective armor. You feel exposed, and less able to control your emotions. The magnitude of what has just occurred in your life has set in. The permanence is screaming in your face.

What I noticed in Missy during this time:

She was preoccupied with worrying about if she was "doing this right?" She wanted reassurance over and over again that she was following the appropriate steps of the grief process. She wanted to get to where she was going - relief from pain - as expeditiously as possible, while following all the rules. She wanted to be the star student and was willing to put in the work to get there.

She was disheartened to learn grief doesn't follow a rule book. There is no formula. It's individual. I was fairly certain she heard me when I said these things to her, but she was thinking "Ha ha, I'll prove you wrong Counselor."

If nothing else, Missy has always been determined to overcome life's obstacles. She knows it's her choice to move forward. This obstacle; however, was going to force her to re-think old strategies, and search for new tools.

Chapter 7

The Sixth Week

*Just as night is
followed by day, so too your dark
times will be followed
by brighter days ahead.*

Karen Salmansohn

Looking back:

In this week I see the woman beginning to take an active part in cleaning up the egg mess. She seeks the advice of experts, asks for help when she needs it, and tunes out those gathered around who provide distractions rather than help. She knows the clean-up is going to be a messy job but recognizes no one can do it for her. She is willing to roll up her sleeves, get out the rags and bucket of water, and start wiping. However, when she peeks to the left or right, she sees others with different but similar messes who aren't moving as quickly as her. She wonders why and second guesses herself.

What I know now:

- Getting back to the things you used to do is scary. Kind of the same scary you get when you try something for the first time. Once you do it, it feels good again.

- Filling the hole your person left in your life with someone else is not necessarily a bad thing. You'll know the difference.
- If you like to exercise, do it! Super helpful.
- I can't say for sure, but it seems those who don't honor a higher power are struggling even more than I am.
- Saying out loud how you feel, as loudly as you can possibly say it, feels really good. Screaming it at the top of your lungs, alone in a car, feels awesome.
- It might seem like what you're feeling is going to last forever. It's not.
- Support groups for survivors don't appeal to everyone.

May 2, 2015

Today I attended the Survivors of Suicide conference with Dr. Frank Campbell as the speaker. I really hate being called a "survivor" and definitely don't like other "s" word. I don't want to be associated with either of them. But since others from the support groups I've been attending planned to go, so did I. Next stop for the bandwagon, downtown Phoenix.

I learned a lot at the conference and left feeling strong. There was a lot to take in and learn. I made notes and left with "take-aways" I want to remember.
Note: For clarity the speaker comments are in bold, my thoughts are not.

- Sometimes we think grieving is supposed to look a certain way. It's not. Everyone does it differently.

- Survivors might experience "post traumatic growth" …learning to appreciate little things. It might be something as simple as suddenly realizing how beautiful a sunset can be. It's easy to get "exhausted" by the grief and stop noticing those little things. I don't think I ever really noticed them in the first place.

- It's possible, and likely, "treasures" will come into your life as a result of the loss. Some people are offended to hear this. It's been just over a month now and I've definitely gained some treasures… deepened relationships with God, family, and friends; new people in my life; being able to easily overlook the little nuisances in life; opportunities to help others.

- The shortest route to insanity is not sleeping. Yep.

- The deceased places a psychological skeleton in the survivor's closet. BUT...it's my choice how I respond to the skeleton.

- Having timelines for getting through grief can set people up for failure. If the expected timeline is too short, people may feel like failures if they don't finish grieving within the allotted time. If the timeline is too long, they may get stuck in grief because they feel they're supposed to stay there when they have, in fact, moved to the next stage.

• **The way we manage grief throughout the process dictates how we will come out on the other end. Potential outcomes are; we will be better than before, the same as before, worse than before, or really worse than before. Each outcome has a different definition. Better than before is "adding something to life in a positive way that was not there before."** It's the only definition I wrote down. The only one I'm willing to accept.

• **Four factors contribute to successful coping: 1) participation in a supportive community, 2) physical well-being, 3) control over daily activities, and 4) having a productive and creative life (getting back to doing things previously enjoyed).** The speaker called them the four legs of a stool. He said they need to be equal for the stool to be balanced.

• **Ideas for dealing with nightmares or recurring thoughts: "Talk it, draw it, write it." Expressing through the various senses activates different parts of the brain. When having a nightmare, take a moment to write it down, or even draw images. Don't turn on the lights to do so, use your non-dominant hand.** Really, that's what he said!

• **Asking "why" does not resolve grief, it's an intellectual distraction from grieving.**

Besides the conference, there were two other notable events today. One was an achievement, and the other was a confusing, and frankly, disturbing event. The achievement...I made it through a day without crying. Yay, finally. I got back to the gym today too. Two achievements I guess. The disturbing event...when I was at the gym I saw a nice looking guy. That's not the disturbing part. I looked to see if he was wearing a ring. He wasn't. I didn't look at him directly, never made eye contact, spoke, nothing. But my instinct was to hide my ring. That's the disturbing part. Exactly 36 days after Scott left, ONLY 36 days after he left, and I'm thinking about appearing unmarried to a potentially single man. I KNOW it was SO wrong. But it happened. I'm not sure what to do with it. I'm confused.

May 3, 2015

I don't know why it's so hard to sit through a church service without crying. Today it happened during the singing. Sit down. Cry for a while. Stand back up and try again. Tomorrow is lunch with Craig and his wife Megan. Craig performed the ceremony. I want to ask him to do something very personal for me. I asked to meet with him confidentially, but he won't. I didn't push the issue. Neil says he wouldn't meet with any woman by himself, even those he knows well. As the pastor of a church, he doesn't want to be seen in a situation that could be misinterpreted. I understand.

After church, I decided to do something suggested at the conference yesterday; try to get back to doing the things I used to do. Scott and I used to have lunch at Famous Dave's a couple of weekends each month. Today I took Mike there. We split a full slab of ribs, and each picked one of the sides like Scott and I would. It could have been weird but didn't really feel weird. Mike is easy to be around. He's not very talkative, I think he's used to being on his own more. Our conversations are sometimes a little uncomfortable for me but I'm so thankful he's here. I don't, in any way, see him as a replacement for Scott. The hole Scott left just doesn't feel as vast with him here. Others might not see the difference in those two things. For me it's a huge difference.

Today I had my first out loud, angry, sobbing conversation with Scott. Driving home from grocery shopping it hit me. I told him how I feel about what he did. He left me in a mess. His letter said something completely stupid like maybe now I could have a good life. Does this new life LOOK like a good life to him? Whatever pain he was feeling couldn't possibly be worse than the pain he put me in for the next 10, 20, 30 years. And our families. And to some extent, his clients and our friends. But they all get to move on. Good job asshole! Look what you did. I'd like to say I hope he's happy, but it's really hard to feel much compassion for him at the moment. So Scott, exactly WHAT about this life is better than before? I said all of this out loud.

Sweet Jen walked over with a delicious meal for Mike and I tonight. Meat, potatoes, salad, and garlic bread. We ate and watched Survivor…another thing I used to love to do but have had no interest in recently. Maybe this is a step in the right direction.

102

Still taking sleeping pills and they're starting to kick in. Tomorrow will be my first flight since that day. Neil will be with me so no concerns about safely. As much as I dislike conducting checkrides, ("a flight test one must undergo in the United States to receive an aircraft pilot's certification"), I'll most likely have to go back to doing them for the money.

May 4, 2015

It was good to fly today. My concern has been being 110% mentally sharp in the aircraft and able to respond to student mistakes, especially any potential emergencies. Neil isn't worried, he says I'll be fine. I'm not sure I'm there yet, but also not sure I'll know.

I met with Pastor Craig and his wife. I wanted to tell him thank you and ask him a question. Writing him a thank you note for everything he's done; coming to my house on "that day", and planning and performing Scott's service, could not possibly adequately express my thanks. I remember very little about "that day," but there are two things I do remember. 1. Vicki, Neil, and Craig praying for me. 2. Craig sitting quietly on the floor against the wall as my world collapsed around me. I don't remember him and Neil coming in, but when I looked over and saw him sitting there, I felt a sense of protection. Even though I've only known him superficially through Neil, when the officers asked who they should call, I asked for Vicki and Neil...and that Neil bring Craig with him. So glad I did.

It was impossible to put any of this into writing, so I told him at lunch. After I told him my memories of that day, I asked him if he would baptize me. Bring a life from a death. I've wanted to be baptized in the past but didn't feel like it would be something Scott would support. Not that he wouldn't support me, because he always did, but for some reason I was uncomfortable with it. My problem, not his. I'm not going to do that anymore. I am committed to making my relationship with God first and foremost in my life. I believe God will lead me to a place where Scott's passing makes sense. It's atrocious, and painful, and something I wish was not a part of me. But it is.

I asked Craig to perform the baptism in private. That didn't fly. He and Megan encouraged me to look at baptism as a time to share with others my acceptance of Christ as my savior. I want it to be just me. Something to share with others at a later time. I understand what they're saying, but I don't know. He asked me to think about a date. This evening at the gym, I had a light bulb go on. I would like to do it on August 10th. It would have been our 24th wedding anniversary. Instead of the day being something to dread, it would become one to look forward to. In 1990, it was the day I gave my life to Scott. In 2015, it will be the day I give my life to God.

May 5, 2015 - 10:00 pm

I just realized today was another waterworks-less day! In fact, it seemed somewhat normal…not that "new normal" thing people love to throw around, just normal. No labels please. It's my normal. Even more encouraging, I guess that's the right word, was I really didn't spend too much time thinking about my situation.

I'm still listening to JO who is tremendously inspirational and encouraging. Move forward, God has plans for me, the "valley" life has dropped me into is temporary. I can be bitter and angry and get stuck in the valley, or I can start climbing up the other side. This doesn't make the valley any less painful, but I do have a choice what to do now that I'm here. It also doesn't mean I'm not acutely aware the gushing tears could occur at any time, in any place, and usually completely out of the blue, by something catching me off guard.

I'm starting to get a handle on finances and how all the complicated details work. New credit cards came in the mail today. Hallelujah. It still upsets me to have to do them, but it's a minor detail. Most things are minor details these days. Life has a funny way of shoving perspective down your throat.

After a week of taking a higher dose of sleeping pills, I'm cutting back tonight. Hoping for two things...sleep and no nightmares. Karen helped me formulate Plan B just in case Plan A doesn't work. Fingers crossed.

Penny to the Rescue and I had an enjoyable, and peaceful lunch today. She and her husband are starting a new business. Yikes! The one thing I can't resist being over the top excited about...starting with nothing, and creating a living, working, growing business. I have to pat myself on the back though for keeping my opinions to myself instead of being all butt-insky. She's doing great on her own and doesn't need my help. But that doesn't mean my desire to chime in isn't there.

May 6, 2015

SOS group was tonight. I'm becoming more and more conflicted about whether or not group is a good place for me. During the first part of the group I was thinking, "last time here." By the end, I felt encouraged to keep going and maybe even try to get to know some of the other ladies. Sometimes the details about how their loved one died is too much for me. I just want to plug my ears, close my eyes, and start singing la la la la. I realize group is not about ME. There will always be things others share I don't want to hear. As I'm sure there are things I say they don't want to hear. My empathy level for a new couple was pretty low. They lost their daughter. She was 35 and left behind 3 young children - one more selfish person to add to my "selfish people list." Three kids? Really? I never imagined myself sitting in a circle with so many people who've been affected by suicide. One more bone Scott threw my way. I guess it wouldn't hurt to start trying to learn their names.

The last couple of days have been good. In fact, I have to admit I spent very little time feeling sad or even thinking about my situation. Is that weird? Is it too soon to be moving on? To be having good days? Should I be dragging around in the depths of sorrow still? How does one know if there's avoidance or healing happening? I think I'm just allowing myself to be me. When I feel sad I cry, mad I get angry, scared about the future I worry, and when I feel happy I just feel happy. I don't even feel guilty about it. Sleeping is even going ok, although drugs are still involved. Cutting the dose last night didn't seem to be a problem. Maybe I'll try this dose for a week and then cut again.

Breaking news: Scott's family is coming apart at the seams. Blaming, denial. Oh wait, nothing new there.

May 7, 2015

Another day passing with not a lot of stressful thoughts about "it." Scott's family on the other hand... The manipulative sister Scott wanted absolutely nothing to do with, and spent less than twenty hours with over the last ten years, wrote a ten-page diatribe of her assessment of Scott's death. She's figured out how and why it happened. In true form, she handed it out to his entire family. Except me of course. One of the family members sent it to me. I skimmed through it...as in SKIM skimmed...enough to know I have no interest in reading the rest. It's not useful or valid in any way. It didn't even deserve the recycle bin. Garbage. Shortly after, I received a well-intentioned rebuttal to the letter from a member of the family. I skimmed it also, only because it's so verbose my head was spinning. I'm sure it's very well said. It's just disgusting how his sister can make a ridiculously awful situation even more ridiculously about herself. Typical. Enough energy wasted on that topic. My prediction is I'll eventually need to cut ties with his family with the exception of Scott's brother, Peter and his wife, Regina.

Interesting thing happened today. When Neil and I were driving to a meeting, he mentioned something about KFC. Before, this would have caused a physical reaction because it was one of Scott's favorite fast food places. But this time it didn't. I noticed it, then noticed it didn't really impact me. Just interesting I guess.

Third meeting with Jill today. I continue to be concerned about days like these when life seems relatively normal. I worry that feeling normal is not normal. Jill says don't worry about it, just "go with it". She'll help me identify if I stray too far outside the boundaries one way or the other. I think she meant excessive grieving on one side of the field, and excessive lack of grieving on the other side. We discussed group and if it's right for me. I'm not sure yet. This is the second time I've heard her say, if I feel more burdened (my interpretation) when I leave than when I arrive, it's not a healthy place to be. When I observe others in their grieving process, I feel as though I'm an inadequate griever. Or that I'm a very proficient avoider. I totally worry I'm not doing this right and about the potential ramifications of doing it wrong.

On a walk tonight, I shared something with Vicki I've been stewing over for about a week. A few days ago, I asked her if we could talk tonight. I needed a few days to get up my courage.

So here it is. I told her about the gym thing…looking at a guy's hands to see if he wore rings. I haven't done that in 27 years and now, 5 weeks after Scott is gone, I'm doing it. I know it's too soon, I know it's completely wrong to even think about a new/different relationship. But I was.

Even worse, I wondered if I should take my ring off so it would appear I'm available. Even worse worse, if I saw a guy without a ring, I subtly tried to hide mine. Pathetic. I'm embarrassed to even write this.

Vicki said it's perfectly understandable I would allow my brain to go there. She said I miss being in a relationship and want to fill the hole. She understands my desire to move on with my life and was encouraging about the things I'm doing to try to make it happen. I reminded her a woman we both know took three years just to move her ring from her left hand to her right hand...and even then, only at the urging of her friends. She reminded me the same woman also still talks to her husband in the shower every morning and has, by her own admission, never missed a day. Maybe it's not good to compare myself to her.

May 8, 2015

Friday again...and I thought time flew before this mess. I met with the accountant again today to continue to attempt to figure things out. One of those things is, exactly how much does it actually cost to have him do what he does? Scott, I sometimes thought, trusted too blindly. Based on the amount Neil is paying his accountant, mine seems really expensive. I can't seem to get a break down of what the charges are for, and what we've paid over the last couple of years. Shouldn't it be a simple matter of pulling up the accounting record and hitting print??

Later in the day, I talked to Neil about feeling like I need to go back to doing checkrides to generate more income. Of course I started crying out of frustration over this one more crappy, and uninvited alteration to my life. He asked how many I want to do each month to feel more comfortable financially? I said, "maybe two or three." Long story short, knowing how much I dislike doing them, he said he'll give me the dollar equivalent of doing two and a half checkrides per month for the next year until I get things figured out. This way, I don't have to do checkrides, but still get paid as though I did. If I want to do checkrides also, then I'll get the normal fee for them, plus the extra money he gives me. Typical Neil. He says deep down I really DO want to keep flying even though I told him a couple of months before this happened, I really don't. Before that conversation, I didn't think so. Now, I'm not sure. We left it that I'll start doing checkrides again. I didn't say this, but I can't see myself taking the extra money. It feels like charity. I don't want charity. I don't want people to feel sorry for me.

Therapist's reflections:

It's a bit unsettling when the water works turn into a slow drip. This slowing of tears may be for a few minutes, a few hours, or even a few days. In the depths of our bereavement, we sometimes pray for the tears to stop. We want to feel as though we're regaining some control of our emotions. Once it happens, we realize we're left feeling confused, guilty even.

I've noticed those who are grieving measure the love they have for the person who died by the numbers of tears they cry. The more they cry, the more they loved their person. Obviously. (I say this tongue and cheek.) Why have we chosen to measure love in such a way? Have we set ourselves up to feel guilty for not shedding a certain number of tears, or for hiding under our sheets for a certain number of days? Should you cry more when you've lost a brother, versus when you've lost a mother? Who came up with this measuring stick? I'd like to meet that person.

Imagine how you would feel if you weren't able to cry at all. The pain is incredible. You can't sleep. Can't eat. Can't concentrate. Yet you can't shed a tear. Does this mean you aren't grieving? That you're not feeling an enormous void in your life? Absolutely not. Grief will look different for everyone!

Stop measuring your grief in tears. Look at your grief as waves. They will come and go. In the beginning the waves will be sizable. They will be furious and come rapidly. At times you may feel as if you barely have enough time to catch your breath before the next wave hits. Although the waves will continue, for longer than you would probably like, they'll be smaller, with more time in between. They'll be less intense, and you may feel more prepared to take them on.

Missy shares that her faith has been an important pillar in her support. She gains strength from her relationship with her faith community, and her new spiritual commitment. It's important to say, this works for some, but not for all. I've seen many who have turned away from their God or their faith after a loss to suicide. They feel God has betrayed them and their loved one. In some cases, even their faith community didn't take a healthy stance on suicide, but instead relied on old and outdated dogma. Suicide is no longer considered a sin. No, not even in the Catholic religion. If you are told otherwise, please walk in the other direction, swiftly!

Turning towards or away from faith is neither right nor wrong. Survivors need to explore what works specifically for them. No one snowflake is the same, nor are we. Those who turn towards a supportive faith (whatever that may be) in a time of loss and crisis, tend to grieve more productively, more efficiently, and feel stronger in their journey along the way.

What I noticed in Missy during this time:

Missy continued to question the way she was processing her grief. This was uncharted territory for her. She was a stranger to trauma, crisis, suicide, and intense grief. Many of us are. Simply put, we don't know what we don't know. We can't begin to understand it until we're in the middle of it. Even then, we aren't sure what's going on.

During this time; however, Missy started to see a sliver of light. She experienced brief amounts of hope. She learned to hold on to those for as long as she could, or at least until the next wave hit. Missy began to realize this level of intensity would not last forever. She began to believe this pain was not permanent. She knew with her faith and this new belief, she could pull herself out and even up. Some day. Hence her post-traumatic growth begins.

Chapter 8

The Seventh Week

*Instead of trying
to change the situation,
let it change you.*

Joel Osteen

Looking back:

What I see this week is the strength the woman had gathered in the previous weeks washed out, lying mixed with the pool of broken eggs. She doesn't see any possible way she can clean up the mess. She grasps at anything to take away the emotional destruction brought on by this recognition. She doesn't recognize herself and is embarrassed by the person she's become. The world she lives in feels completely foreign to her. It's the little things. Things that used to draw her attention are unimportant now, while other previously unnoticed small details, unrelentingly scream for her attention. She spends a lot of mental energy remembering how beautiful the basket of eggs used to be, and how they used to make her feel. She finds herself looking away from the mess they've become, focusing her thoughts instead on how she can replace them with a new basket filled with beautiful new eggs. She knows it's wrong to think like that but it's all she can do at this moment.

What I know now:

When you're hurting or feeling hopeless, and there's no one available to encourage you, having a media or written resource to turn to 24/7 is irreplaceable. For those who prefer to read, perhaps a book or website. For those who like to listen, a pod cast or radio station. And of course, there's always TV for those who like to watch. It doesn't matter what it is, as long as it inspires you and gives you a sense of hope, or even the smallest boost of courage you need to take the next step.

Two primary resources served to comfort me during this early time. One was a book titled "Jesus Calling." Every page is a different day of the year consisting of a short motivational narrative and related scripture. The other resource I couldn't get enough of was the Joel Osteen station on XM radio. At that time, I was grasping for anything I could make sense of and give meaning to. I remember no matter what I read or listened to, it was as though it was meant for me. Exactly what I needed, when I needed it. As if someone knew where I was headed and preplanned the scripts.

Regardless, both resources were stabilizing factors in my life for quite some time. I made the list below as I listened to one of JO's sermons. The title of the sermon is "Living Content." These are key ideas from the sermon, in my words, as best as I understood them at that confusing time.

These are key ideas from the sermon, in my words, as best as I understood them at that confusing time.

- Discontentment will follow you everywhere you go if you allow it to. Decide to be content and enjoy life. It doesn't happen automatically, contentment is a choice. This doesn't mean give up on your dreams, have them, but trust God's timing.
- You don't grow in the good times, you grow when there's pressure. Instead of trying to change the situation, let it change you. Bloom right where you're planted.
- Train your mind to see the good, be grateful for what you have. You may have a thousand reasons to be unhappy, find one reason to be happy.
- Try to be satisfied with where you are right now. It doesn't mean you'll settle there, it means you won't live frustrated always wanting something more. Have faith and trust in your spiritual beliefs.
- Learn to enjoy the simple things in life. We tend to think, *I'll enjoy life when...* you fill in the blank. Focus on what's right in your life, on what you do have, not what you don't.

May 10, 2015

"I hate you Scott." I actually said it out loud today. I feel guilty, angry, overwhelmed, confused, beaten down, different, desperate, lonely, scared. EVERY single one of those is because of the cowardly thing he did. The shithole my life has become is his fault. Screw him. Before this I was happy, confident, comfortable, excited about the future, protected, part of a team. Now I'm not only trying to create a plan for the future, I'm scraping to simply figure out today. Planning, listing, and organizing are ways

116

I gain control over what's happening. But how can I do any of those things when day is now night, yesterday is now tomorrow, right is now wrong? It's like looking at one of those reverse image photos where the colors are all flipped around. You can still see the picture, but it's way off. And not reality.

Yesterday Mike and I visited our parents for Mother's Day. It was an exercise in putting on a happy face. The minute we got in the car to drive home, I started bawling...the stress just came out. My mom started to cry as we drove off. We're all pretending, protecting everyone else. Scott's absence is not just an elephant in the room, it's the entire continent of Africa. I know we're all just doing the best we can. Doing it differently probably isn't an option at this point in our lives.

The bad evening got worse when I had to call the airlines. Still trying to get a refund for the tickets to Europe for the Greek cruise scheduled for July. Princess Cruises had no problem cancelling, but the airlines are complete tyrants. After having to explain the situation to two different people, I was told by a third I have to go on-line and submit a request for refund. Along with a copy of the stinking death certificate I can't bring myself to even look at. Forty-five minutes later, after scanning the death certificate as I peeked through one partially open eye, I sent it to the airline along with my explanation. It felt more like begging. The reply? My "request will be reviewed" and I will "receive a decision in 7-10 business days." Hello complete lack of compassion. Oh, and by the way, since the credit card Thieves cancelled the credit card I used to make the reservation, there will be a further review.

Church this morning was all about Mother's Day. Many times during the sermon I had to bite my tongue hard to avoid crying. It was about women "being the wind beneath" their husband's wings. That stung. Why didn't I hear these messages earlier, why wasn't I a stronger wind beneath Scott's wings? Why didn't he ask for help if he was struggling?

I'm two people on the inside now. The one I used to be is battling the one I've become. Sometimes the old me pulls ahead, other times the new me takes control and drags me back. She needs a name. How about Mouse. I'm like one of those multiple personality people. That's freakish. Missy the Strong vs. Missy the Mouse. Who will win today, this hour, this minute?

May 11, 2015

The yoyo-ness of this is killing me. Up, then down, then more of the same. It's exhausting and every now and then a good cry seems to release some of the tension I can usually feel building for hours. Tonight, it happened at the gym. While I was working out my mind wandered to times in the past when I would get there first and Scott would walk in later. I thought about how much I wanted him to walk through the door today and smile at me, like he would. Tell me my muscles were getting bigger, like he would...no one to notice that now. I had to leave without finishing my workout. Cried all the way home.

I talked to Karen about my frustration with Mike recently. On top of being overwhelmed in general, sometimes I seem to have to take care of him also…buy everything, cook dinner, clean up. He helps when I ask but doesn't take initiative. She reminded me he's not really capable of being a care taker so I'm expecting too much. It's just misplaced anger, sadness, etc.

When I told her about possibly traveling to Kauai in October with my friend Maureen who would be attending a veterinary conference, she encouraged me to go. Scott and I met Maureen at a conference in the Galapagos Islands. If we go, she'll attend the conference during the day, and we can hang out together in her off time. If I go it will be seven months after he died. I think I'll be ready but not sure…how do I know? It's a few months away. Scott and I were supposed to go to this conference together. Kauai is our favorite Hawaiian Island. We were looking forward to eating coconuts from the ground in our secret grove. Fucked that up too didn't you? Just one little treat after another keeps coming my way compliments of my lovely, caring, committed, husband. Yes sarcasm.

May 12, 2015

I don't know what to do, I feel like I'm sliding down a long, ugly hill, and gaining momentum. I've cried several times a day the last couple of days. Feeling less hopeful that I can piece together a happy future. I just miss having someone who's here with me, a part of me. I guess this is what it means to feel lonely in a crowd. It's really depressing and sad. I feel like I'm constantly on the edge of breaking down. Even flying today was difficult. My mind kept wandering to Scott and the things we used to share together, but never will again. Is it even possible to establish a relationship with someone else? I know people get married again and live happy lives…I just can't envision it right now. But I spend a lot of time wondering how to make it happen.

Another thought has become a constant. The vision of his last act happening. The final moment. I HATE that and fight it back every time I start to think about it. But I can't help it, it just keeps coming. I don't want to ever think about it.

Last night when I was walking, a neighbor pulled his car up next to me and said, "Hey Missy." I thought he was going to say something like, how are you doing, do you need anything, etc. You know, all the thoughtful things the other neighbors say. No, not him. He wanted my apricots. He asked if I was going to pick them off the tree in my front yard. He said the birds are getting them. I told him I'm waiting for them to get ripe. He said, "Oh they're ripe, I've been eating them." Then he flipped his thumb toward his wife and said, maybe I'll send her down tomorrow to pick them, so the birds don't get them all. ARE YOU KIDDING ME?!?! I was too stunned to say the apricots were Scott's favorites and I like driving in every day, seeing them on the tree. I would rather let them all drop to the ground and get scavenged by birds and bugs than have him pillage a tree that reminds me of Scott. This morning I called Jen in hysterics and asked her to explain the situation and tell him I don't want him to touch my apricots. She lives next door to him and was offended at what he'd done. She said, "He needs to keep his grubby hands off your tree." I'm sure he didn't mean any harm, it was just thoughtless.

"Come to Me all of you who are weary and burdened and you will find rest for your souls." From Jesus Calling today. My soul needs rest. I've never been so emotionally exhausted, feeling like there's no reserve to pull strength from. Just completely drained. Something weird happened when I was brushing my teeth getting ready for bed tonight. I looked in the mirror and saw the physical me. That part of me has become invisible behind the big ball of wrung out emotions. When I saw myself in the mirror, it's like I became a real person. A real person who's capable of using this body and brain to manage the emotions. Maybe just another freakish game my mind is playing to try to push through all the pain. To convince myself I can do it.

May 13, 2015

I finally gave in to Karen's request to consider taking medication during the day. Last night I woke at 3:00 am and had two terrible hours, finally took some melatonin at 5:00, then slept until 8:00. The last few days have been just a complete roller coaster of bad and badder. When I'm not crying, I've been on the verge of it. I called Karen this morning for help. She and Mike worked together to set up an afternoon appointment with one more medical person who was previously not a part of my life…a primary care physician. Karen and I met with him today, me in person, her on the phone. So glad she was "there" to explain the situation. I hate having to. It was bad enough that I had to answer the "Marital Status" question on the new patient form. Having to check the "W" box is just cruel.

The doctor prescribed something for me to take during the days and says I can still fly. A lot of pilots take it, according to him. He says it will help the extreme swings smooth out a bit. He and I are both minimalists when it comes to medication so we're a good fit. Later, when I was talking to Peter about my resistance to taking medication, he helped me feel better about it. He said if you break your leg, you need crutches for a while. The drugs are a crutch to keep me upright while my mind begins to heal. Makes sense.

I met with the EMDR therapist for the first time this morning, we just talked, info-gathered. The EMDR will begin in a few sessions she said. She asked some hard questions like, did I know why he did it, or have any indication he was going to? How did he do it? All those things I don't want to think about, much less talk about. She offered me a weekly session, rather than every other. I sobbed through most of the hour. She probably thought the original plan of biweekly was inadequate. She says the F word a lot, which I must admit I've used quite freely in the last six weeks. Regardless, it made me uncomfortable and I told her. She was very good about saying she would refrain from saying it. She said I might have to remind her.

Last night when I was awake for those two hours I started looking on the internet for Meet Up travel groups. Singles. It seems so pathetic, like something only people without friends or partners do. I guess I'm one of those people now. Scott and I loved to travel. I have a fear it's come to an end. I know I'm nowhere near ready to get involved with these groups. Something about just knowing they're available is comforting...or is it a desperate attempt to try to cling to something that was yanked away from me? Then I read Jesus Calling...

"When things seem all wrong, look for growth opportunities. Especially look for areas where you need to let go, leaving your care in My able hands." Perhaps being able to travel again is one of those areas I should let go and not try to control. Besides, I'm supposed to focus on dealing with each day as it comes, not the things I feel I've lost. There's enough present loss to deal with without piling on the future loss as well.

May 14, 2015

Another SOS group tonight. Turns out, most of the group is either taking anti-depressants now, or did in the past. Some burned through many different ones before they found one that worked for them. It's very depressing to hear that some, who are years past the horrible day, are still taking drugs. That's not my plan. Sleeping pills...pretty common. I guess when it comes down to it, since I take a sleeping pill at night and something during the day, I'm technically under the influence at all times. Isn't that just swell?

Today was better than the last few. I only cried in group vs. off and on all day long. And I didn't slam the door in any of the instructors' faces today. Probably need to apologize for the other days. I wonder if they understand. I think when people see me having good days, they're confused when a bad day or string of bad days comes along. Doubtful the improvement today is about the medication. According to the experienced users, they can take a couple of weeks to kick in. Probably another one of the up and downs I have.

I've been concerned I should write thank you notes to all who've helped, contributed, or reached out in some way over the last few weeks. I asked the group if they did...they were split. Some wrote them and some didn't. They all agreed though, it's perfectly ok not to. They said people don't expect it. Not sure if I agree. A couple of people even said it was "therapeutic" for them. Definitely not something I see happening for me. If I do them, it's because I feel it's the right thing to do.

I have a flight test scheduled for tomorrow. I hope it's one of the "good" days. "Good" these days is anything better than totally crappy. I'd have no problem cancelling the flight if I didn't feel fit to fly, but I don't want to have to cancel on a student. They get all psyched up to do their test. It's a bummer for them when it doesn't happen for one reason or another.

I've noticed I've become much more patient and less stressed by the little things. Guess that's a little itty bitty positive in this cluster. For example, things like a rescheduled phone conference between the attorneys and the insurance company, and the interesting way Mike unloaded the dishwasher (big forks wedged into the little fork slot) were complete zeroes on the scale of who cares.

May 15, 2015

"Or maybe your marriage didn't work out..." From JO's sermon today. Well, no, it really didn't. That's exactly what happened, my marriage didn't work out. I had a plan of how it was supposed to look all the way until we were old and taking care of each other. He had other plans. Now the chalk board has been completely erased. I've been thinking maybe my situation is more comparable to a divorce than to a different type of death such as an illness or an accident. In both a divorce and suicide, someone made a decision to leave the marriage, and the partner was left to slog around in the mud and aftermath of the other person's choice.

On our walk tonight (slopping through pouring rain with umbrellas) Vicki told me about her divorce years ago. Her husband left her, completely against her wishes...and then filed bankruptcy which she was sucked into. In addition to losing him and having the financial matters to manage, she lost his family who she was "in love with." Much of how she felt during that time is how I feel now. She went to a divorce group where she met women who'd been attending the same group for years, in one case, 16. It was her first and last group because she decided it was not going to be her 16 years later. During our conversation I had an epiphany. Perhaps the reason group can be so depressing sometimes is it's filled with people not willing or able to move forward. Maybe those who've been able to more successfully move through this process are no longer in group??? Maybe those still in group think they want to move on, but really don't because they are gaining something from staying in their current situation, as bad as it is.

It's been a successful completion of day two of round the clock dependence on drugs to get me through the days and nights. What a proud moment. The most emotional part of today was driving to the downtown post office to put a letter in the mail before the last pick up. Mike had a job interview today. I really want him to be successful at his job search. For two reasons; one, so he can experience success, and, two so he'll continue to stay with me…not necessarily in that order. Earlier in the day I sent out a prayer request to 20 friends asking them to pray for him to get the job. He would be embarrassed if he knew I did that. After his interview I helped him compose a thank you note. I even wrote the card for him because his handwriting is beyond abysmal. On the way to the post office to mail the letter, I started praying/bawling to God. I said, *please please please let him be offered this job.*

Last thought for the day, again from JO. "I may be knocked down, but I'm not knocked out."

Therapist's reflections:

The stream from the faucet can turn from a drip to a wide-open gusher in a matter of hours for a Survivor. All grief is intense; however, grief from a loss to suicide is considered "complicated grief." Complicated grief is unpredictable.

As we've stated before, grief isn't linear, it comes in waves. Many of us have heard of Elisabeth Kubler-Ross'

126

Five Stages of Grief: denial, anger, bargaining, depression, and acceptance. I once heard it said, before her death, Elisabeth shared regret for ever printing her theory. She said people had confused her meaning of the stages. There was an assumption the five stages should, or would, come in order, and once you had completed one stage you would neatly move on to the next. To the contrary, Kubler-Ross was simply providing framework for different emotional waves of grief. There was no specific order to be followed, denial didn't always come before bargaining. Instead, Kubler-Ross explained we may experience bargaining first, then denial, then back to bargaining, and so on along the way. The five stages of grief were never meant to propose a step-by-step progression, they were created to help us frame and identify what we may be feeling. When it comes to grieving a loss to suicide, there is no timeline. There is no right or wrong way. There is only YOUR way.

What I noticed in Missy during this time:

Since day one, Missy exhibited the ability to think outside of the box when it came to her healing. She was willing to try different resources, groups, and techniques to get the relief she needed to care for herself. During this time, she was open to, and attempted, a specialized technique for trauma called EMDR (Eye Movement Desensitization and Reprocessing). After finding a therapist who specialized in this technique, Missy found this particular therapist wasn't for her. Missy didn't feel emotionally heard; therefore, didn't feel emotionally safe, in this new relationship. It was apparent to Missy early on, this therapist was probably not versed in suicide loss and its complexities.

Missy was already experiencing a bit of an identity crisis during this time. "Am I the person I was before the suicide? Or am I someone completely different now?" She didn't want to hear the phrase "new normal" and we know she certainly did not want to be typecast. Adding a new and vulnerable relationship with a new therapist at this time might not have been a good idea.

Look for those professionals who have experience with suicide loss. If it doesn't feel right after two to three sessions, it's not a good fit. Don't force it. This is an important relationship. If you don't feel respected and understood, the therapeutic relationship will not work.

This is also true for a support group setting. Whereas typically support groups specific to suicide loss can be quite beneficial for some, they aren't for all. For some new Survivors two sessions in a group setting may be all they need. Others may benefit from this type of support for years. As I referenced earlier, there is no right or wrong way, there is only YOUR way.

Chapter 9

The Eighth Week

Take a deep breath,
pick yourself up,
dust yourself off,
and start all over again.

Frank Sinatra

Looking back:

Here I see a woman who has changed. Situations she could previously handle without a problem, are mountains for her now. It's as though someone has put her old pictures in new frames, just different enough to cause her distress. She needs assistance to accomplish even the most basic of tasks. She spends a significant amount of time worrying about how she'll handle new situations. As hard as she tries to just go about her business, the mess of eggs lying at her feet is not going away. She feels like each time she attempts to take a step forward she slips in the mess and falls. She is hateful toward the one who made this mess, but at the same time wants him with her, to hold her hand and love her.

What I know now:

- When you select an individual counselor, make sure he or she has experience working with clients who've lost someone to suicide. Those who aren't experienced in this area are as lost as you are as for how to proceed. They're not a good match for your situation.

- Rely on people. Rely on people. Rely on people.
- You are making progress! Don't worry if it feels like you're not, it's just hard to see it in the moment. You'll eventually recognize it when you look back later.
- Do the best you can to take care of yourself physically, even if it's difficult.
- Everyone is telling you to try to focus on the present and not the future. It's easy to say that but it's DIFFICULT to do. Just try. You might get it wrong most of the time, but when you get it right, it will make those moments easier.
- If you feel sad be sad, if you feel angry be angry.
- If you feel lonely reach out.
- When you feel happy, just enjoy it.
- Take long deep breaths. It's calming.
- If you watch for the little treasures each day offers, you'll be amazed at how many there are.

May 16, 2015

What a weirdly "normal" day today has been. I experienced only a few teary moments (as in welling up but not streaming down my face). Randy went with me to the nursery to get my dead peach tree dilemma resolved. The tree died shortly before Scott did, he had started the process to get a replacement under the guarantee. Randy took over and got it all worked out while his young daughter, Tanner, and I walked around looking at trees and enjoying the beautiful flowers. Next, we went to the farm store…like normal people. Then to lunch…like normal people. At the farm store I bought a decorative stepping stone shaped like a dragonfly to go under the new peach tree. It's Scott's tree, he's the one who wanted it. A dragonfly had a special meaning for us. One of our hobbies was Letterboxing, a treasure hunt requiring us to figure out clues found on-line. Our code name was TwoTall and our stamp was a dragonfly. Although I've ugly-cried buckets in front of Randy many times, I was glad he and Tanner were on the other side of the store.

Second teary moment was at lunch when Tanner drew a lovely crayon picture for me. I was overwhelmed by how the entire family, including the pre-teen children, has cared for me through this ordeal. I told Randy how much I recognize and appreciate it. He says it's a privilege for him to serve me. He's such an inspiring example of a Christian. We talk about faith a lot.

This evening Mike and I went to a graduation party for a kid who used to live next door. Other neighbors were there as well and we all sat in a circle and chatted. I felt like a normal person doing normal things. People in the support groups have said they feel guilty about having a good time. I don't. The group facilitators also seem to promote the idea that I'll eventually feel guilty. I wonder if some in the groups take on those feelings of guilt because they've heard they're supposed to? I feel a lot of ways about a lot of things; but at this point in this voyage through hell, I can't imagine feeling guilty about actually having a good time.

May 17, 2015

Today was busy but fairly normal. I tried a new church…still can't seem to make it through a service without crying, or at least having to hold back tears at one point or another. I hung out at Starbucks by myself for a couple of hours and talked to Karen for a while. She's considering applying for a new job and asked for my opinion. It felt good for someone to ask me for help instead of being the one always asking. Maybe she was trying to help me get back to myself, or maybe she really wanted advice. Either way, I enjoyed being a giver instead of a taker. I'm back to thinking about moving forward with the home care business.

Later I talked to Maureen. We began making plans for the conference in Hawaii. A couple of aspects of the trip concern me…traveling by myself scares me, staying in a room with someone other than Scott…will I have patience and tolerance? Will I be able to emotionally handle being there with someone else when it was supposed to be Scott? It isn't until late October so there are a few months left to get these things under control. I felt most excited when Maureen said we could be "travel partners" in the future. She's single and loves to travel like I do. She can afford to do trips I like to do. I'm feeling very positive about this. Losing the ability to travel has been a huge worry for me…maybe this is the solution. All the normalness of this weekend is making me nervous.

From the outside looking in, I think I'm doing better overall. Is it the passage of time? The drugs? The counseling? Church? Supportive friends? Or a combination of everything? Or just a temporary false sense of progress that will blow out the window during the next crash? I think I've lost, or am losing weight, nothing drastic but something to pay attention to.

I've been getting to bed later and later. If I go to bed at what used to be my normal time, I wake up too early and can't go back to sleep. The bad thoughts come and won't let me sleep. Early morning is when they're the loudest. It's been easier to go to bed later so I wake up later. I'm getting same amount of sleep, just not the ugly mornings. Night times are definitely not as bad as the mornings. Odd random thought…I used to sleep without clothes for no purpose other than it was comfortable. Now for some reason, I feel compelled to sleep with them on. I really don't understand why.

May 18, 2015

Did I think much about Scott today? No, can't say I did. Good thing? Bad thing? Neither? Could the drugs be kicking in? If they are, is it ok that I didn't seem to spend much time grieving today? Only time I got a bit choked up was having coffee with friends Wendy and Roger, telling them about the opportunity to travel to Hawaii in October. It's always the random things.

I unloaded on one of the mechanics today after he told an instructor to "Pull the fucking helicopter in" in front of a customer. Not appropriate behavior in any circumstance, but a really, really bad idea when the instructor's boss is one tap away from shattering into a million pieces. It was not a nice chewing out. Later I wondered how much of it was really about the mechanic's behavior, and how much was the anger I feel about what Scott did and what it's done to my life.

May 19, 2015

If I'm supposed to feel something other than anger towards Scott, I guess I'm not there yet. Running from morning to bedtime to get everything done, crying almost non-stop for seven weeks, living with someone who's 180 degrees different than what I've been used to for the last 25 years, taking medication night and day, worrying about finances, modifying my lifestyle to accommodate those finances, meeting regularly with accountants, lawyers, doctors, financial advisors, group and individual counselors, having to patch together a plan to maybe salvage the business we spent a lot of time and money creating and were scheduled to launch on June 1, battling the airlines to get a refund for tickets to Europe for a cruise that isn't going to happen, battling Scott's former employer to get the tiny life insurance they agreed to provide, and fighting with a hunting organization to get a refund for the $2,500 hunt Scott had, unbeknownst to me, paid for but will not be going on, IS NOT MY IDEA OF A BETTER LIFE. The one he somehow seemed to think would magically appear for me when he did what he did. What a moron.

Let's not forget completely disrupted sleep habits, waking up about every two hours to pee because the medication I'm taking is making me so thirsty, and feeling very, very alone in this world especially when things are

134

not going well and I just want him to talk to. Of course, there's the constant worrying about what my future will look like once all of the above problems are figured out. Yeah, bonuses all over the place.

I'm nervously moving forward with my plans to go to Hawaii in October. I found a potential condo so I'm planning to make plane reservations tomorrow. Next decision...first class seat or back of the sky bus? Probably back of the bus...that sucks. Yes, another vast improvement in my life, moron. Well don't I sound like a whiner? I would say yes if I was a midget and could actually FIT in the back of the bus seats but I'm not. I'm 6'2" and being crammed into a space designed for a malnourished six-year-old child for seven hours is just one blood clot away from the emergency room as far as I'm concerned.

May 20, 2015

Is time going in fast motion or backwards, I can't really tell. I feel like two people, the one who has it figured out and is moving forward with life and the one who continues to struggle daily with the sadness and overwhelming-ness of it all. This morning I was crying before I even got out of my bedroom and can't even remember why. Later, I was still trying to get some personal matters taken care of then work started pulling me a hundred directions at the same time. My parents have taken over battling the airlines who've agreed to refund the airfare but insist they have to return it to a closed credit card account. People, it's closed!

I saw Tina the EMDR therapist and again cried through most of the session. Still no EMDR. She said the F word three times until I said, "stop using that word." It sounded rude, so I added "please." She did tell me to remind her after all. I was feeling so overwhelmed by not only the sadness, but everything I have to take care of. Still feel I can't get everything done, yet at the same time I've taken on planning the trip to Hawaii and still stewing over how I can get the home care business going. I woke up at five and couldn't go back to sleep so that didn't help.

I've been craving sugar. Wonder if it's stress? The medication? On the way back to work after seeing Tina, with my red eyes and streaky face, I stopped at Paradise Bakery for a cookie. Got a dozen. It made me feel better to sit there eating my favorite cookies with others instead of by myself. They each only had one cookie and I, without any shame whatsoever, ate two and thought about having a third.

SOS group got on my nerves tonight, it was dominated by the same three people. Mostly the blond girl whose abrasive and screechy voice makes me wish for earmuffs. The leader is a nice guy, too nice. Sometimes he lets the group run wild, the same people take over and won't stop talking. I think he needs to redirect, include others who get pushed aside. One member, Suzanne, I'm starting to like. Even though she talks a lot she sometimes has good things to say. She's one of those people who is easy to incorrectly prejudge. One of the women in the group is a nurse and sadly, instead of feeling concern for her loss, my first thought was wondering if I could use her as a connection for my home care company.

May 21, 2015

Tonight at the gym there was a young couple, in their mid 20's I would guess, who were bickering over the silliest thing for about 30 minutes. He wanted to go somewhere with his friends, she had a problem with it. It made me so sad to watch something so trivial getting in the way of their relationship, I had to choke back tears several times during my work out. As I was leaving I went to them and said, "You obviously care about each other and I just wanted to say my husband died a couple of months ago and I hope whatever is going on, you can find a way to work it out." I planned to say more but then I started crying. Then she started crying. Then I bolted out the door like a complete idiot. Way to make a scene. I felt I had to say something. People argue over the stupidest things!

I used to think I wanted to counsel people who lost someone to suicide or be a part of the team that goes out in the community to offer support shortly after a suicide has occurred, like the team that came to me. Not sure I want to anymore. I really just want to leave this behind and move on, it seems like joining the team would be paddling to the other end but still staying in the same pool. I'm sure I'll change my mind several more times.

JC (Jesus Calling) said to watch for little "treasures" today. When I walked into the gym tonight, entire sections of the walkway were covered in beautiful yellow flowers fallen from the trees overhead. Golden treasures.

May 22, 2015

This morning Mike told me he has to go back to Chicago for a week to help prepare his condo for sale. He might have to stay "a few extra days" if his doctor says he needs a small procedure. I had a meltdown. He assured me he's coming back. I can't say these drugs are helping much. It seems I'm on the verge of tears almost all the time. Then in typical Mike fashion he gruffly snapped, "You have to understand I have to go back to take care of some business." He's been thrown into this situation where he's in way over his head and unfortunately doesn't really know how to interact on a sensitive level. Even though I try to appreciate him for who he is and understand his limitations, I fail most of the time.

I'm panicking. Trying to figure out how I'm going to handle Mike's absence. Do I go somewhere? Ask friends to stay with me? Ask them if I can stay with them? I have the pets to consider. I can't abandon them. My friend Sue lost her husband five years ago to illness and never had anyone staying with her, not even one night. She's confident I'll be fine and able to handle it. I guess I'm just not feeling strong or confident about the situation because my mind is running through all sorts of potential options. Staying alone isn't on the radar.

Diane, told me her roommate who owns the house they all live in, is planning to sell it this summer. NO! That can't happen! She's become my walking partner and huge part of my support system. OMGosh if she leaves… I have to find a way to keep her here.

Therapist's reflections:

Week eight and the shock and denial previously mentioned has more than likely completely fallen away. You feel as though you're standing naked, fully exposed. Not only is it uncomfortable, it's tiring, and frightening.

About this time, you might start to feel as though you're a burden to others. You tell yourself they don't want to hear your story anymore. You label yourself a "Debbie Downer."

While it's true many won't know how to relate to your loss, there are people around you who genuinely want to help, to listen, to be present for you. Yes, even months later. Keep the small handful of people close to you and focus on being more accepting of their assistance. Have you ever considered it might help them to help you? Your support system is feeling out of control, too. They want to provide relief for you but may not know how. There isn't a rule book for either party, Survivor or Support System. They are following your lead. Although you don't feel like much of a leader at the moment, when you minimize your pain or your needs they have no additional information to rely on. You are not a burden. Keep those who get it close to you. Cry on their shoulders over, and over, and over again, until there are no more tears to cry. It helps them help you.

Anger may be more prevalent right now. Or, you may not be angry at all. I have noticed there is a misconception with suicide and anger. You don't have to be angry at your loved one (although it's perfectly acceptable if you are) you can be angry at the situation, or the mental illness, or the world in general. Your life has been turned inside out. Anger is an important part of this grief! Often we assign shame and guilt to our feelings of anger, "How can I be mad at my Mother for leaving me, when she was in so much pain?" Allow genuine emotions as they surface, without labeling them. I saw this quote a while back: "I sat with my anger long enough until she told me her real name was grief."

What I noticed in Missy during this time:

In the weeks after Scott's suicide Missy was filled with judgment. Maybe this was how her anger was presenting itself. Eight weeks out Missy continued to take a stance she "wasn't going to be one of THOSE people." Almost defiantly. She wasn't going to be a weeping widow years later. She wasn't going to be one of those Survivors who needed prescription assistance, not for more than a few months anyway. She wasn't going to be one of those people who put their life on hold because they couldn't deal with it. She wanted to be the exception. I've worked with Missy for some time, from her initiation into this "group" no one wants to be a part of. As much as she wanted to avoid so many of those potholes on the road of grief, to be different from the "others", Missy instead experienced so much of the same, and hit nearly every pesky hole in the road the "others" had. She just needed to kick and scream about it first.

You will receive advice about this grief process from other Survivors, or professionals, either in a group setting or one on one, or while reading through book after book. If the advice received doesn't feel like a good fit, don't push it away and throw it into the trash can. File it away. Odds are, some day, at some time, those words may ring true for you and then you can say "Oh yeah, they said this might happen!" I'd rather you be prepared for what could be in your future, than to be struck to the ground feeling uneducated and unprepared when a scary wave of emotions or behaviors hit. You've already experienced shock and surprise once, don't set yourself up for it to happen again.

In retrospect many of the things Missy was avoiding presented themselves in her life anyway. At least she could access her file and say, "That's right, I heard others experienced this," or "Jill said this might happen." This education was key to assuring Missy she wasn't going crazy or doing anything wrong. She was grieving. Education is power - go get yourself a filing cabinet.

Chapter 10

The Ninth Week

When we transport ourselves out of the pain,
we miss all of our transformation because
everything we need to know to become
the people we were meant to be
is inside our loneliness.

Glennon Doyle

Looking back:

This woman still struggles with everything she has struggled with since she discovered the broken eggs. Continued difficulties and apparent lack of change is all she can see most of the time. When she's able to step back and look at her situation from a distance, she sees some sort of order beginning to take place. The basket of broken eggs is still a complete mess, very little of it has been removed. But at least there's a small hint it's being sorted into smaller, more manageable piles. In addition to cleaning up the egg mess, the woman voluntarily takes on other tasks. Completing these other tasks is within her capability. Doing so gives her a sense of accomplishment. Putting her energy toward them; however, is counterproductive. It further drains any energy she has.

What I know now:

- It's good to have goals. Don't let anyone convince you yours are not legitimate.
- Sometimes it helps to temporarily put those goals to the side while you deal with more pressing matters.
- When you feel overwhelmed with everything you need to get done and don't know where to begin…just pick one thing and do it.
- You might notice a pattern. Maybe some days are more difficult than others. For example, weekends, or the day of the week your person died. It's helpful to preplan activities for those days. Lunch with a friend, a movie, an appointment.
- The house-full of friends, family, and well-wishers has probably dwindled by now. Take the initiative to stay in contact with them. When I needed to talk to someone, I rotated who I called to not burn out any of them.
- When you need emotional support or help with something, ask someone.
- Remember to show your gratitude and appreciation when someone helps you. Who doesn't like to feel appreciated?

May 23, 2015

God has a plan for me. I just have to listen. Mike will be leaving for a week and I'm panicking about staying alone.

The home care business remains on my mind. I need a partner and believe Dr. Cheryl is the right person. She lives in California. Since we need to sit down anyway to discuss our expectations, goals, assumptions, potential conflict resolution etc., I asked if she could come next weekend to sit and discuss those things. Oh, and since my brother is so selfishly leaving me alone, can you babysit me while you're here?

Cheryl is awesome. Within two hours of my email, she had a plane ticket to arrive on Saturday, the day Mike leaves. She'll stay until Wednesday. He'll come back Thursday unless his Dr. needs him to stay longer to deal with his heart arrhythmia. I feel better now since most of the time, including the weekend, is covered. I'll have to figure out the rest later. As only God could plan it, Cheryl's daughter, who lives in Prescott is having a birthday on Monday. Cheryl can spend the day with her, and I can keep a planned lunch date with my friend Suzi. Suzi and I had a bit of a falling out months ago and haven't seen each other since. I'd like to see if we can work things out. Cancelling the date would not be a good start to a reconciliation.

Mike took the initiative to buy and cook fresh chicken on the grill tonight! What a nice surprise. With each day, comes a greater realization of my new responsibilities. I'm slowly understanding if I don't do something myself, or ask someone else to do it, it's not going to get done. Changing light bulbs and smoke alarm batteries, folding sheets that have been sitting in the dryer for a week, garbage and recycle in and out on the right days, informing the gardener a particular sprinkler head has pooped out, removing the annoying and useless solicitations from the front porch, scooping cat litter boxes, washing pet bowls, opening mail, tending to the hot tub, and on and on and on. Having Mike take the chicken initiative without me asking really made a difference. It made me happy. Perhaps I should tell him. I don't think the permanence of what Scott did has completely set in. I'm so angry he would put me in this position. What a fucked up life he created for me.

May 24, 2015

I realize feeling overwhelmed is partly my fault. I've purposely taken on things I don't need to…locating a condo in Hawaii for Maureen and I in October, focusing on pushing the home care business forward. If I took those two things out I wouldn't feel so used up. But also, I wouldn't feel excited about the future. Having something to look forward to helps me keep going,

Sometimes I feel like having Mike here is becoming work…but I also like having a body in the house. I don't feel like I gain any emotional support from him and not a lot of task-oriented help either. And he certainly isn't contributing financially. He needs to get a job soon and if that happens, we'll have a discussion about how he can contribute.

May 25, 2015

I heard two quotes today that really struck a chord. From the Walking Dead: "The pain doesn't go away you just make room for it." And from a movie, The Woman in Gold: "You have to let her hate you so she can heal."

It's been another day of feeling crappy and on the verge of crying pretty much all day. I was cranky with the pilots several times...the five I hired literally the day before this happened probably think I'm a total bitch. It's really all they've seen of me so far.

I met Wendy and Roger at the movie theater. We parked in separate lots and met inside. Even walking to and from the theater by myself sucked big time. I can't imagine the rest of my life being like this, but it's how it feels...like this is the rest of my life. As good as it gets.

When I got out of the helicopter today, the first thing I did was check my cell phone. For a brief moment I wondered if there would be a text from Scott, like there often was when I landed in the past. Nope, this is as good as it gets.

After the movie, Roger and Wendy came to my house so he could do some minor house repairs he'd offered to do a couple of weeks ago. They're man things. I don't have one of those any more. Sitting on the floor, talking with Wendy while Roger worked on the gate latch was a good distraction. I eventually come back around to complete sadness, anger, frustration, worry, feeling overwhelmed. Distracting myself only works for a little while. A horribly ugly Ferris wheel has become my present and future. Ride to the top to see the pretty views, descend back to the stink of the dirty fairgrounds.

May 26, 2015

Plain exhausting. That was today. I had to fly twice then spent nearly an hour crying with Jill. Again, I felt strong walking in and about two minutes later dissolved into tears. Lack of sleep doesn't help. I woke at 4:30 after having a nightmare and couldn't go back to sleep. In the dream, Scott had a girlfriend and wanted me to meet her. She was young, 16 I think, short, chubby, dark-skinned, with long dark hair…about as physically opposite of me as possible. In the dream I was so angry with him and he was completely cold, indifferent to my anger. He was laughing because I was upset about his girlfriend. In a car I was trying to poke him in the cheek with an umbrella, but he just kept dodging it and laughing at me. He had absolutely no remorse for his actions.

Feeling alone in this world seems to have emerged as a theme in my sessions with Jill. I feel so sad. I'm surrounded by friends who reach out to me, who I can reach out to, yet there is a big, huge, gaping, missing component. It's having that one person in life who knows me well, is always there for me, is my partner, and is the one I go to when I need a little whatever. My person isn't here anymore. Many people can provide small parts of these things…but all wrapped up in the same package? No. Gone. I can't see myself living like this for any extended period of time. It doesn't work for me. Dogs are pack animals, cats are loners…I guess I'm a dog. I need my pack leader back.

May 27, 2015

Small victories to celebrate: Attending first session of EMDR, getting a refund from the elk hunt Scott prepaid, and noticing I wasn't bothered by eating dinner on the couch watching TV by myself. The last one was really hard, but I did it. Jill said reading this journal may eventually serve a purpose for recognizing progress. I'm not ready to read it but at least I saw that small progress today. Baby steps.

The EMDR session today was another sob session with Tina. Weird thing, this EMDR. It's definitely something I would have scoffed at if I heard about it before this mess. I guess when you're feeling desperate you're willing to try anything. I hold onto gadgets as they alternate buzzing in my hands. Following Tina's hand with my eyes as she moves it back and forth? Really? This helps? To be continued...

Tomorrow will be the first morning I have to wake up early to be somewhere. So far, I've had the luxury of waking when I wake - really nice with such restless nights and much less sleep than I need.

May 29, 2015

I'm running a million miles an hour. And need to go faster. The last couple of days have been non-stop trying to keep up with everything. It's been a good distraction but still there are sad and angry moments every day. Sometimes I can't even identify the cause. At a pilot conference yesterday, most of the other helicopter pilots "knew," but everyone tip-toed around me. The only one who said anything about Scott was an airplane pilot I know from a committee we're on. I think people are uncomfortable to bring it up. Fortunately, the guy who saved me a seat knew my extreme desire to sit in the back of the room. He kindly saved me the very back corner. BEST seat in the house! The helicopter pilots tend to migrate to the back of the room so I had friends around me.

Therapist's reflections:

You may notice the desire to stay busy. This actually is fear of slowing down. The thought is "If I run in circles long enough, I'm bound to get exhausted. Then there won't be space or energy to feel, really feel. My hope is I will drop from exhaustion at the end of the day, to sail off into a mindless sleep. Only to do the same thing again tomorrow." And the result? Does it help? Temporarily maybe, but long term you discover speeding up, only to avoid the pain of slowing down, is just delaying the inevitable.

A remarkable therapist explained the pain from suicide loss like this: View this pain as the Boogeyman. You know, the type of Boogeyman you see in the 1980's horror films. Michael from Halloween, or Jason from Friday the 13th. In the films, these characters make our skin crawl. They lurk and linger outside the house. You peek at them from behind a curtain in your living room. Even if you can't see them, you know they're out there, somewhere. You're always on high alert! Most choose to either hide behind the couch or run upstairs to lock themselves in a dark closet with no exit. Despite all your efforts he always ends up in the house, waiting to pounce when least expected. What if you went to the front door, opened it, and invited the Boogeyman to come in? Whoa! What if you took control of the situation? At least as much as you can? Odds are, as the story goes, the Boogeyman is going to make his way into your home either way. Wouldn't you like to gain as much control over the situation as possible? Maybe even try to reason with him a bit?

What I noticed in Missy during this time:

A couple months had passed by now and the stream of visitors and well-wishers was definitely slowing. Missy not only missed Scott, but she was beginning to feel genuine loneliness. This loneliness seeps into places others may not be able to understand. Grocery shopping may be hard for some, it was a chore done together every Sunday. Going out to eat becomes a challenge. Table for one? I don't think so. What about parent-teacher conferences or Mother's Day tea for children who've lost a parent?

Missy experienced the feeling of loneliness while walking into a movie theater to meet friends. She could have been surrounded by her entire support team, in a theater filled with 300 movie goers, all with the same goal, but she wasn't with her partner. She was a plus one. A perfect example of how you can be in room of people, and still feel alone.

Chapter 11

The Tenth Week

Be still and know that I am god.

Psalm 46:10

Looking back:

As a result of her inability to resolve the egg situation, this woman focuses on a different project. It's a good break from the emotional overdrive she's been in for over two months now. It brings some normality back into her life. It gives her a sense of control over her future. A sense of control torn from her grasp when someone upset her basket and crushed the eggs. She notices others around her seem to be returning to life as it was before, even though she's still standing in the middle of the egg mess. She leans on those who support her goals and has had to let go of others who bring negativity into her life. She feels ok about cutting those ties. The woman begins to cautiously admit to herself she's able to breathe on her own - without someone holding the oxygen bag.

What I know now:

- It's really hard to listen to people complain about trivial things. They do, all the time. Just let it pass, it's not worth your energy. Remember, before you

151

lost someone and gained your current perspective, you might have done the same.

- Don't worry if your emotions seem highly unstable. They are, it's normal.
- Surround yourself with people willing and able to positively contribute to the path of healing you're on. This includes friends, therapists, family, co-workers, neighbors.
- Trust the people you've selected. Thoughtfully consider any guidance they give you. You selected them for a reason.
- You'll lose friends in this process, maybe even close friends. But you'll gain many more than you lose.
- If you discover someone is causing you more grief than support, gently escort them out of your life - at least for now.
- If you attend recovery groups, identify and connect yourself with others in the group who are moving forward. Ask for phone numbers, invite them to lunch or a movie, invite them to call you if they are having a rough moment.
- Above all, keep reminding yourself you WILL find joy again.

May 30, 2015

I was having one of those weepy days when it seems almost anything makes me cry. Sad things, happy things, nostalgic, just looking at something with no apparent connection to anything. On the way to work I stopped at Carl's Jr. for my daily iced tea. As I was leaving with my tea, I saw two guys sitting in a little tiny bit of shade being cast by the shopping center monument sign. They were supposed to be twirling and flipping one of those pointer signs, trying to attract people to a particular business…I guess they were on a break. It was really hot. It made me cry that they had to be out there doing such a crappy job, so I went back to Carl's Jr. and got them each an iced tea. They were so thankful I started to cry about that too. OMG I'm totally not an emotional person but everything is a hot button these days. I hate being like this. So out of control, never knowing what to expect and when.

Mike left today. After dropping him off at the airport, I went to Starbucks to wait for Cheryl to arrive. It was another of those moments I felt so alone in this world…even though I just dropped my brother off, and only had to wait an hour to pick up my next babysitter. It's so hard not having one special person to call about anything, even just to say… "Hey, just dropped Mike off and I'm sitting at Starbucks now. Ok bye". I miss that so much.

It occurred to me, putting so much effort into planning and restructuring a new life for myself is completely wearing me out. It's actually causing more stress. Maybe I should have planned to be alone for the week to see how it goes. I didn't. Cheryl arrived as planned and has been a pleasure to have here. We caught up with each others lives and talked about the home care business, how/if we could make it work.

I asked Vicki to "pop" over to meet Cheryl so she could give me an honest opinion as to her partnership potential.

Vicki commonly "pops" over to give me her opinions on people, so she did. I'm curious to hear what she has to say.

May 31, 2015

I haven't been interested in writing as much lately, it seems like my days have been lists of events...went to church, went to lunch, cried about this or that... blah, blah, blah. Is this a good thing? A bad thing? How do I know?

I'm still trying to patch together some type of future. Perhaps it's not the right time. Spending a lot of time plotting and planning is a good thing in the sense it's distracting and hopeful. But maybe a bad thing in that I'm hiding from the complete upside down-ness my life has become. Defense mechanism in full bloom.

Cheryl and I spent a fair amount of time talking about doing the home care business together. She's the perfect person to partner with but I'm getting the sense the tasks I would need her to do aren't the tasks she's interested in.

June 1, 2015

Just another crappy day. It started off bad and got worse. Nothing really even happened I can identify as the trigger. A couple of days ago in my daily reading from Jesus Calling it said, "press back the demands pushing in on you, create a safe space around you, a haven in which you can rest with me." The next day said "I look into your mind and see your thoughts spinning round and round going nowhere, accomplishing nothing. All the while My Peace hovers over you searching for a place to land." Yep, lots of demands pushing in. Lots of spinning round and round going nowhere.

I've tried to push away all the stress and things pulling me in every direction, to stop my thoughts from constantly being on my future. The future no longer there. I know I should quit trying so hard to fix it…to repair my broken life. But I'm a fixer. I can't sit and wait for something to happen. When things aren't going the way I want them to, I change them. I can't change this situation. It's such a helpless, depressing, hopeless, and desperate feeling. I try to "press back" all of it to make space for God, to let Him be the fixer. I'm just not being successful at it.

Today I had to do full downs with a student today. It's the riskiest flight maneuver they have to learn. We simulate engine failures and then end up on the ground. Only Neil and I teach it. The instructors are required to stop the maneuver and "make a recovery" before they get to the ground. Weirdly enough, I was able to "press back" everything in flight most of the time, at least in the critical moments. I imagined putting all my worries and problems outside the helicopter, on the other side of the window. Maybe I can pretend I'm flying when I feel the world crushing in on me…which is all the time.

However, after the flight, I could hardly wait to get the student out of my office to close the door and cry for about an hour before meeting a "friend" for lunch. I think she may be the first friend who becomes a former. I've heard some friends no longer work out as friends when faced with this situation. I have to admit, sitting at lunch, listening to her bitch about her job and surgery recovery, and how much trouble she's having with her employees, I felt like getting up and walking out.

Then it really got disturbing, she gave me, what felt like, a prepared speech on why I shouldn't have been upset with her actions a year ago. She said she's under so much pressure and her work environment has "just been hell" for her. Are you kidding me? You're going to lecture me right now? About how hellish your life is? At this particular time? The first time I've seen you in about a year? You attended Scott's service so it's not as if you don't know what happened. Seriously? Normally I would have tried to discuss and explain, but I totally didn't even care. She could have said anything at that point with absolutely no reaction from me other than to politely smile, nod, and act empathetic to her situation. ACT being the operable word.

At the end of the day, as I was walking out, Neil came in and sat down. Already on the verge of tears, I just wanted to get out of the office before I broke down. Didn't happen. We spent about an hour talking. He tried to explain even though life has changed for me, I have a good future ahead of me. He said it's going to be a "bloody ugly battle" to get there, but I'll get there. I told him at this point, there seems to be no relief from the constant pressure and ugliness. And there's certainly no goodness in my future. He reminded me of the bullseye he drew on a stickie for me a couple of weeks ago. In the middle of the bullseye he wrote May 13th. When he drew it he "guaranteed" me things would be better next year on that day than they were this year. He said I should at least make it until then or I'm "going to miss something cool."

Tonight is the first time I've gotten into bed with no one else in the house. No one here to take care of. No one here to take care of me. I'm not sure how I feel about it. Cheryl is coming back late tonight after spending a long day with her daughter.

June 2, 2015

Boing, the mood ball has bounced back to the sanity side of the net. It's unreal how quickly and unexpectedly my moods change. I wish: A) they would stop, B) they would become more predictable, and C) I could identify triggers that cause them to go one way or the other. I would like a large serving of option A, with two side dishes of options B and C, please.

Regarding being alone last night, in hindsight, I must admit, it wasn't as awful as I anticipated. I was even a bit relieved to not have to entertain, or care for anyone.

Mike told me he's been offered a fulltime job in Scottsdale. It was a job he really wanted so I'm super happy for him. I'm also happy for me because it means he'll keep living with me for now. Not sure how long I'll be happy about this but for now I am. Karen said at some point he and I need to have a discussion about him contributing financially. I wouldn't even know where to begin in determining a fair contribution.

June 3, 2015

Tonight will be the first time I sleep all night in my house alone since the day Scott left. It doesn't feel terrible…but I am unusually restless and wide awake. It's 11:15 pm. Mike is coming back in three days.

The SOS group has gotten huge, there's a lot of side chatter and not a lot of group discussion with so many people. There seemed to be a bit more happiness and people finding joy in their lives. One woman, who lost her husband about five months ago, said her son is scheduled to move in with her. She said she's just started to enjoy living alone and isn't sure she wants him there. She was also able to look at wedding photos with "warm feelings" for the first time. Another woman, who lost her husband six months ago, thinks she's going to be happier in the future than she was before. She says it's because by recognizing how fragile life is, she's begun to live life fuller. Do I feel ok about living alone? Get warm feelings looking at wedding photos? Think I'm going to be happier in the future? No, not really.

My mom called while I was at work and left me a weepy voice message saying she knows I'm home alone and she's thinking about me. It's SO hard to talk to her when she cries…it's hard enough to keep myself together without being her support system, too. I'd rather she go back to our normal conversations about food and what she made for dinner. Superficial, but at least no energy required to listen to her describe each dish she made.

Karen also called to find out how the home care partnership talks went with Cheryl. I don't think we really came to any conclusions other than our logistics (her being in California) are difficult to work with. We left it at a point where we'd both keep putting thought into options. I think she may be interested in pursuing the same business with her daughter in Prescott. Karen said she'd like to be a part of the business and come down for a couple of days each month to do the marketing. I don't think it's enough, but perhaps better than nothing, at least a way to get started. I have to think about what it would entail, what my time commitment would be, and how I could work it out with my current job. I think Karen is looking for something new, so this might be exciting for her. In a couple of years when her youngest son graduates, who knows where it could go. Just one more thing to ponder. Unfortunately, these ideas have jumped on the merry go round spinning around in my brain. Perhaps part of the reason I'm still awake now…at 11:34pm.

June 4, 2015

People can be so clumsy with their words. I can't honestly say I would be much better…however having gone through this, I certainly think I have a clearer perspective on what to say. And what not to say. But what works for me, might not necessarily work for others. This day had mostly a normal feel to it.

June 5, 2015

Not sure why I'm so restless in the evenings these days. It's 11:15 and I'm not even close to tired. Just took my lovely sleeping pill so that will change…but without it, not sure when I might feel tired.

I've had four fairly normal feeling days in a row after the Monday disaster. The way things change from day to day is mind boggling. This morning started out feeling like it may turn into "one of those days" but I consciously made an effort to not let it. Listened to JO, focused on work, touched base with a few friends, had lunch with Amy from group. She's doing well and doesn't want to "dwell." But she was pursuing a divorce from her husband when he died. A bit different dynamic. She's minimized her group attendance because she feels like she takes backwards steps when she goes. Being around people who've recently lost someone tends to take her back to her early times. A place none of us want to go ever again. It could be a problem for me in the future. Dwelling is not my plan either.

Funny thing happened during lunch. Amy doesn't know it yet, but she became a potential partner/employee in my home care business. She said she's ready to get a job since her kids have gotten older. She's been offered one with an insurance company but isn't interested due to lack of potential for growth and movement up in the company. She wants to do something and "see how far she can take it." OMGosh, perfect for what I'm trying to do. Take the ball and run with it. More for the merry go round, isn't there a seating capacity?

160

Mike gets back tomorrow with five boxes of stuff. Not sure what the heck to do with it all. Making space for him means moving some of Scott's stuff out. I'm not sure I'm ready to face this particular event yet. Maybe shuffling it around and cramming it into other places will have to be the plan for now.

I'm also not sure how I feel about Mike coming back. Surprisingly, the last couple of evenings by myself have been somewhat relaxing. Knowing my personality; however, I'll get bored quickly if this goes on for too long. The aloneness in the house this morning, getting ready for work, felt sad. How do people do this thing, living alone??? Perhaps this is why the day started off feeling like it was going down that road.

Living alone means having absolute and complete control over everything that happens in the house. It also means absolute and complete responsibility. It's a trade-off and, at this point, I'm not sure which one fits best for me in these circumstances...having complete control or having someone to share responsibilities.

Therapist's reflections:

The last half of your biography was ripped from its spine, the pages thrown away, on the day you lost your loved one to suicide. Grievers can fill their minds with clutter, frantically attempting to recreate some type of order, to reassemble those pages from their book. The effort to find

161

immediate order is a knee jerk reaction. An act of desperation. But it's natural.

Busying the mind during this phase, running around to fill time and space, and attempting to make plans to carry you to the end of time, are efforts to avoid intense pain. A couple months out from this loss you may believe you're ready to rewrite the last half of your biography. If you write it, then you'll have something to focus on. Goals to work towards. A target. However, it took twenty plus years to write the first draft. Don't rush the new edition. You're a different person than you were before, don't be surprised if your story takes on a whole new shape.

This is hard to hear, but I truly believe there's something positive to gain from this loss (I know! You may not be ready to read this. Just tuck it into the filing cabinet for later.) The positive thing? Perspective. You've gained a new perspective on life. It's clearer now what really matters. It's even more clear what doesn't matter. Things like grocery store chatter, conversations about the latest blockbuster movie, and last night's sports scores, seem so trivial. Listening to friends talk about stressors at work, or yet another story about the Royal Family, make it challenging to relate. You now have a much greater understanding of what really matters in this world: family, friends, health, faith, breathing, love, memories, connection. Not the house we live in or the car we drive. Not even money.

As your perspective shifts, so will your interests. In some cases, your friendships will shift. What you need from a true friend may look different. That's okay! It doesn't mean there's anything wrong with you, or you're less of a person for not being drawn to the same people and things you used to be. You are transforming. Life is about growth. Sometimes this comes to us in the most painful ways. It's okay to shift your interests. It's okay to end old relationships and develop new ones. So much is changing - your perspective being first and foremost. Don't attempt to re-write your story just yet. Let it develop over time before you pick up the pen and force it.

What I noticed in Missy during this time:

Missy vacillated back and forth trying to decide what was helpful to her and what was not. I saw this often when it came to her participation in support groups. She had a lot to say about the other participants and how they were processing their grief, yet she still hadn't figured life out for herself.

She had difficulty relating to other Survivors at times. This is normal. The cause of death may be the same, but the story behind it never is. Yet, she found positive attributes in those she was quickest to judge. At the end of the day, Missy was thankful for her new posse. She may have complained about attending supports groups, yet something kept pulling her back into their circle. At least there, she knew she wasn't alone. At this time, knowing that was invaluable.

Chapter 12

The Eleventh Week

Living is a form of not being sure,
not knowing what is, next or how.
We guess.
We may be wrong,
but we take leap after leap in the dark.

Agnes de Mille

Looking back:

The woman standing over the broken eggs has begun to admit to herself the constant self-imposed distractions aren't going to serve her ultimate goal of cleaning up the mess. The distractions provide temporary respite and create space to breathe...but bring her no closer to resolution. She's become stronger in her convictions of the steps she needs to take, but at this point, is only able to point her feet in the right direction. Convincing them to move is another thing. Even though she's not ready to take the first step, she's starting to feel momentum building. This is, in part, because she realizes the life she's constructed for herself to accommodate the egg mess isn't working. She's ready to start distancing herself from it.

What I know now:

- Sadness, anger, and other difficult feeling will come rushing toward you at unpredictable times. Just be

164

aware of this and be prepared when they do. They will pass.

- I think it's normal to feel guilty, like you missed something that would have stopped the suicide. Even that you're responsible. I know I certainly did in the beginning. To this day, I still think I could have been a better wife...but isn't that true about anything in life? To think we could have done it better? I definitely no longer feel responsible, or guilty, or like I missed something.

- The randomness of good and bad days is extremely frustrating.

- Learning to make decisions you're not used to making is a process. After you've done it a few times, the confidence will come. It gets easier in the future.

- Severe grief changes people. Relationships within the immediate family may be unstable during this time.

- Those who weren't as close to the deceased tend to move on much quicker than you'll be able to. They expect you to keep up. Remember, the deeper the wound, the longer it takes to heal.

- Recognizing there's something you need to do, and actually doing it are two separate things. Take the time you need.

- Speak your mind! You might sound harsh but some things need to be said.

June 6, 2015

Mike's back. As I expected, I have mixed feelings about it. Totally surprising since when I first found out he was going to leave, I panicked. Not sure what to make of it. Karen suggested I think of him as a roommate…go about doing my own thing and don't think of him as a "companion" in any way.

Today was good until late in the day. I started feeling like it was going downhill and could spiral into what I'm now calling "Red X" days. Those are the really terrible days. I put a red X on the calendar to track them. The last "Red X" day was June 1st. Weird how five good days is considered a success. I tried to figure out why I was feeling one coming on…because Mike is back? Because I didn't listen to JO at all? Because I talked to my dad who sounds completely depressed but like he's trying not to? Because my mom, when describing her bad day of golf said, "but I won't feel sorry for myself, I'll feel sorry for you?" Because Vicki had to cancel our walk (disappointment)? Because my TV is having connection problems (frustration)? Because because because. Lots of maybes but no answers. Maybe there is no reason. Having this many good days makes me worry the next Red X is coming.

Things improved when I went for a three-mile walk and had an hour long conversation with God. I think this is what it means to have a personal relationship with God. Instead of thinking things to myself in my head, and trying to figure them out, I addressed Him…asked Him a lot of questions. Then when I answered myself, I heard His voice instead of mine. I even mumbled out loud sometimes. As a result, I actually felt better by the time I got home.

11:00 pm again. I've really GOT to figure out a way to get to bed at a reasonable hour.

June 7, 2015

Lesson of the day: Picking out the cheesiest Doritos is pointless when I'm the one who will have to eat the other ones later.

It was another busy day. A day I purposely filled with stuff. A day I purposely avoided other stuff. I went to church, then Starbucks with Sarah, cruised around a farm store with Penny to the Rescue, walked with Diane in the evening, then talked to Laurie until about 10:30. I filled in all the empty cracks by percolating over how to get the home care business going. Here we are, nearly 11:00 again. I've worked very hard to fill my time which I'm not sure is a good thing. Perhaps it puts a barrier between me and processing Scott's death.

I'm starting to worry I've had too many "good" days in a row...ie. not disasters. It can't possibly be over, so the question is, when is the next monsoon going to roll over the fragile little city I'm rebuilding?

June 8, 2015

Crazy *"epiphalogy"* today. That's an epiphany and an analogy squished into one idea. At church on Sunday the substitute pastor compared a story in the bible to an airplane on final approach for landing. He said when you make a nice smooth approach, you'll have a nice smooth landing. Later I found out he's a pilot for Virgin Airlines. Now it makes sense.

Today in counseling, Jill made a smooth approach resulting in a smooth landing. We made a written list together, and at the end of the session she asked, "Can I give this to you?" Not, "you keep this", not "you should take this and read it", not anything directive in nature. WOW, totally smooth approach. It puts the control in the client's hands. Result: smooth landing, client (me) feels in control during an otherwise massively out of control time in life...which made me think back to the sermon...which resulted in the epiphalogy.

The Epiphalogy: A smooth healing process (approach) will result in a smooth future (landing). However, in aviation, unexpected situations invariably arise. There will be un-forecast turbulence, Air Traffic Control never fails to throw a curve ball, and failed equipment sometimes requires trouble shooting. But a good pilot strives to use good Cockpit Resource Management (CRM), the effective use of all resources available to her at any given time. Yes, my pilot is a girl. If I apply this to the healing process, I want to use all the resources available to me to deal with the unexpected situation (Scott dying), to move forward and be successfully at the end. Smooth approach, smooth landing.

The list Jill and I made today is an inventory of the things I recognize myself doing to heal, and those I'm doing to hide/avoid dealing with the situation.

Doing to Heal: Focus on my Faith, walk with neighbors, attend counseling with Jill (general) and Tina (EMDR), attend SOS groups, journal, talk to friends, read Jesus Calling, listen to JO, tapping technique, use lavender scents to relax.

Doing to Hide: Spend too much energy getting the home care business going, over schedule my time to avoid alone/thinking time, take medication morning and night.

If someone asks me what it's like to deal with the aftermath of suicide, I'll refer them to the computer game Tetris. In the beginning the multi-shaped blocks fall from the top and pile up until there's no more room on the screen. You lose quickly...many times. Then you start to learn the game, how to rotate the blocks, how to shift them into place, and every now and then you fill up a row and it disappears making more room at the top for the falling blocks. But eventually you make mistakes, create gaping holes and incomplete lines that don't disappear, the blocks pile up, and you lose again. Then you get better at the game and you can juggle the blocks even as they begin to fall faster. You learn to do other things like talk on the phone at the same time. You feel like a pro. Until the game gives you a block that no matter how you rotate and shift it, it just doesn't fit neatly into the row. Eventually you lose again, but at least you spent more time playing than losing. By that time, you're a much better player. Something that was once difficult is now easier - but there will always be difficult spots. You'll always have holes in your game. You become ok with it.

June 9, 2015

My brain was sucked dry by my sister in law. I really don't think the conversation we had for the last 63 minutes is healthy, or productive. I'm concerned how it's going to affect me. She's so venomous toward Scott's parents and sister, and just rants non-stop. I couldn't put a stop to it. Once, about 40 minutes into the conversation, I said, "I'm going to change the subject now because I'm not interested in talking about this anymore." We did briefly, then she wound it right back to the same topic. I don't think it's an overestimate to say her mouth was moving for 53 minutes of the 63 minute conversation, and most of it was angry. I'm already worried I've had too many good days in a row. After listening to her spit poison into my brain, I'm even more worried about crashing in the near future. Why did I allow that?

Tina sent a text to confirm our EMDR appointment tomorrow. I texted back I wanted to cancel. She asked if I was ok. I answered I would be there. I'm sure she's totally confused by this exchange. I guess I am too. I think I'm feeling counseled-out right now. Appointment with Jill yesterday, appointment with Tina tomorrow, SOS group the following night. I think I need to keep going for now…I just don't know how to be sure.

So many decisions to make. Before, I never had to make them on my own. Scott was always here to discuss them, especially the financial decisions. It's a scary place to be, suddenly responsible for my own future. I suppose I always was, but at least it felt like someone had my back when I was confused or unsure how to proceed. Now it's just me. The feeling is a strange combination of control and confusion. Completely uncomfortable.

I'm awed and humbled by the people who've stepped up to be there for me in this situation. I've seen sides of people I never knew existed. I've had to show them sides of me I hoped to never have to show anyone. Neil, Randy, Karen, Vicki, Jennifer, Jen, Mike, Kim, Sarah, Bobbie, Amie, Sue, Hunter, Floyd, Zilda, Sotero, Cindy, Laurie, Dr. Cheryl, Maureen…the people I knew pre-madness, who've reached out and become a much bigger part of my support system than I could have ever hoped. There are also the additional blessings who've become a part of my mess, those I've met during this process I wouldn't have otherwise …Diane, Penny, Pastor Craig, Sheryl, Roger, Wendy, Jan, Amy, Suzanne, Hollie, Jill, Tina, everyone in the SOS groups. There's only one who stepped down, and very possibly out of my life. Scorecard: Stepped up: 20. New positive additions: 12, plus groups. Stepped down: 1. God has been good to me in the support system category.

June 10, 2015

Not a Red X day…but not one of the good ones I've been having either. It started with Mike's lack of ability to

171

communicate or even be present in a conversation. Since he's not working and has really nothing to do all day besides go to the gym I'm paying for, go hit range balls, and go walking in the park, I asked if he could go grocery shopping. He was sitting on the couch doing absolutely nothing except reading the newspaper. So, when I asked him to go shopping and he responded with a grunt, not even taking a second to look up from his...my...paper, I became a little irritated. The conversation went like this:

Me: "Here's the list...Almond Coconut Silk milk, it's in the..."

Him: Grunting, "I know what it is."

Me: "...cold section. Eggs, Greek yogurt like this one." Me holding up a yogurt container he doesn't even look at.

Him: Interrupting, "You mean coconut flakes?"

Me: Exasperated, "You're kidding right?"

Him: Grunting, "I'll find it if it's on the list."

Me: Walking out the door.

Him: "Was that 12 eggs or 18?"

Me: Still walking out the door. "It's on the list." Close door.

Imagine my surprise when he came home with a mutant version of Almond Milk instead of the Almond Coconut Silk I asked for. And I didn't check, but I bet there's a new bag of coconut flakes in the kitchen somewhere. Splendid, add it to the two other bags in the freezer from my granola making frenzy last year.

Before heading home tonight I asked Neil for guidance on how to best handle the situation. He reminded me I probably can't expect much more from Mike considering the position he's put himself in in life. He said to try to remember all the good things about him being here. He's right, there are a lot. I'm a bitch.

When I got home I was friendly and respectful and didn't mention this morning. Not worth it and he doesn't deserve it. I imagine I'll know when it's time for him to move out. For now, I'm ok taking the good with the bad…today was definitely the bad. He's great to be around when he's in a good mood and I enjoy having him here. I just wish I saw more of the good mood.

Jesus Calling yesterday said "look at other people through lenses of love." That's what I'll do with my brother.

June 11, 2015

Suicide. How does society even begin to address a problem of this magnitude when sometimes there are no apparent indicators, no predictability, commonality, or logic? Answer: it can't. It struck me tonight, sitting in group (all two and a half long painful hours of it) that the group was so incredibly diverse. Blue collar, white collar, artists, former addicts, convicts, type A and B personalities, those who walk with God, atheists, those in poor physical condition, athletes, intellectually gifted…and those not so much. The only commonality is we all live in the US, a civilized country. Do the bushmen of Africa have this problem? I would guess not. Each member is a valued and important part of the tribe, essential to its survival. Maybe that's a commonality, whether or not the person has a sense of importance and feels valued?

I am so saddened I didn't do a better job helping Scott feel valued. I think he felt he'd let me down. He had, but WTF? Suicide? I value him SO much and realize it so much more now than I ever did. I was a crappy wife when it came to letting him know how much I appreciated him. I wish I had a second chance to show him, to make him feel like the king he was. But now it's me suffering. I guess I'm getting what I deserve.

Mike was in his room with the lights off when I walked in at 9:15. A bit unusual for him, I hope he's not drinking. Or on the verge. It's been a problem for him in the past. He's been moody the last couple of days. Maybe stressed about his move to Arizona? The new job? Living with me? I should talk to him but conversations with him are difficult. He appears to be challenged in the communication department. I think avoiding problems, and even conversations that might lead to problems, has been his default mode for many years. It's easier to ignore the problem and remove himself from the situation than to have a discussion. I guess we're both situation-avoiders. I think tomorrow I'll initiate a conversation to check in, but I don't want to step all over his comfort zone. He's supposed to start his new job next week.

June 12, 2015

Today would definitely qualify as a Red X day. Neil and I met over lunch to discuss the meeting we'll be having with my accountant Earl next Tuesday. I'm concerned about the amount I'm paying him. Neil is concerned some of my investments appear to be losing a fair amount of money. By the end of the conversation I was in a complete panic about finances. Again. And once again, Neil was good enough to sit with me for an hour discussing it. Poor Neil has had to deal with so much of this.

In between tearful outbursts, I joked I just need to find a rich man to marry. He totally shocked me by actually agreeing. I had to laugh because I didn't expect this reaction from him. His requirements include, Christian, rich, and over 50. So funny. He even suggested I go online to locate the aforementioned Christian, rich, 50+ year old guy. He didn't like my plan to support myself in the future with a home care business, thinks I'm just making a move out of fear. I told him I have to have a plan for my future, no one else will do it for me. If he ever sells his business and I end up unemployed, I'll need a way to make a living. There aren't really many local companies in need of helicopter pilots. *Would you like fries, soda, or perhaps a helicopter flight with your burger?* We're not exactly a versatile lot.

Then there were the pet problems today. Brownie has been vomiting and didn't eat dinner last night. Baby has been peeing tiny amounts multiple times a day. I took Brownie to the clinic today and Dr. O will come to my house tomorrow after work to look at Baby...if I can manage to catch her. It just doesn't stop. If Scott were still here, he would have handled this. It's what veterinarians do. It's what he did. It was his part. More and more of his part that I now have to figure out. Decisions to make. He completely left me in a mess, so poorly equipped to handle any of it. I feel like I'm starring in the TV show called "Naked and Afraid." Oblivious, unskilled, naked people dumped in the wilderness to survive with no apparent tools. At least they have a partner to work with. And they know the show will eventually come to an end. My partner quit and there's no end to my show. Yep pretty crappy day.

Therapist's reflections:

No one is ever prepared to experience a loss to suicide. Even if a loved one attempted multiple times in the past. We either think, "He would never do that to me!" Or "He'll snap out of it! We'll get through this. He's overcome problems in the past, he can do it again."

This loss is sudden. It takes you by storm. You aren't prepared. No one can ever be prepared for this type of loss. As a result, the shock of this death can strip you of any comfort and faith in the world you had the day before. It can leave those left behind on edge and waiting for the next shoe to drop. After all, life wasn't supposed to happen

176

this way. You had plans for the future. Now all of that has changed.

Waiting for the next wave to hit, or the next tragedy to occur, is common. Fear of the unknown has become a reality. Often Survivors begin to function with a heightened sense of alert - by the U.S. security code standards, a new Survivor operates under code orange at all times. They are awaiting the next attack, whatever it may be. For some it may be paranoia - fear that your children won't make it home from school, or your boss is going to call and fire you tomorrow. In a Survivor's mind, whatever it is, can cause a lot of anxiety and add to the exhaustion.

Closing in on the three-month mark, I see Survivors begin to really come out of their fog. Begin is the operative word. At the same time, they're mentally and emotionally exhausted. Whereas, they may have been functioning on auto-pilot before, relying on help from the people around them, now mental and emotional fatigue starts to set in. Day to day grieving is exhausting! I liken it to running a marathon, each and every day!

Not only are Survivors fatigued, they're scared, anticipating another tragedy might be looming around the corner. If not a tragedy...a complication, a difficult decision, or a meltdown. This is a normal reaction to sudden loss. Thought patterns can become irrational and untrusting. Survivors aren't sure who or what they can trust anymore. Consistent positive experiences, and time will help you to regain your confidence in the world again.

What I noticed in Missy during this time:

Blame. Regret. Punishment. Missy would replay her last conversation with Scott. Telling herself she should have said this, or responded with that, or stopped nagging about this... She'd convinced herself she was an unloving spouse, and at times underserving of Scott. This was the story she'd created to punish herself, to lay blame on herself.

At this time in her grief, she was unable to hear others when they would point out this thinking was irrational; that she was in no way responsible for Scott's suicide. Missy needed to come to this conclusion on her own......and she would, when she was ready to digest it and own it.

Chapter 13

The Twelfth Week

Sometimes life subtracts,
sometimes it adds.

Dexter

Looking back:

What I see is the woman with the broken eggs accepting the necessity of putting her future plans aside for now. She realizes she needs to clean up the current mess first. She feels a low grade, pervasive sadness, perhaps resulting from this acceptance. As she attempts to focus on cleaning the mess, she finds herself being pulled away by immediate responsibilities. Some of the tasks were previously her responsibility, others are new. They come as a direct result of the dumped egg basket. They are tasks, in some cases, involving caring for others. The woman feels mentally and emotionally ill-equipped to manage these new tasks, even under good circumstances. Even the tasks she capably handled in the past are difficult now. She manages them in the only way she can, she asks friends for help. They respond and she's grateful. It's tremendously uncomfortable for her to have to rely on them.

What I know now:

- Even after three months you'll continue to discover things that are different than they once were. Things you had not yet realized would be. Don't worry, eventually they all smooth over.

- Deal with your loved one's belongings ONLY when YOU are ready. Don't let anyone convince you "it's time." I got rid of a couple of things I later regretted letting go. FYI, three years later, most of his clothes still hang in his closet. It's no one's business except mine!

- Don't worry if you sometimes feel you're all about you. You must care for yourself if you're going to care for others.

- In the beginning I though he killed himself to hurt me, he didn't. I realize this now.

- If you find something you believe helps you move forward in your healing, try to stay consistent with it.

- If something or someone is holding you back from moving forward, let it (or them) go.

- Don't worry if things that used to interest you no longer do. One of two things will happen, either they'll eventually interest you again, or it won't even phase you that they don't. Either way it's a win.

- You might feel gloomy for no obvious reason.

- Things that earlier made you completely fall apart might still make you sad, but they won't have the same powerful impact they did in the beginning. Make a point to notice when this happens. Acknowledge it doesn't hold the power over you it once did. Even though they might feel like baby steps, they are awesome achievements!

June 13, 2015

It was one of those puffy eye mornings. Not just because I had morning face. I decided to take Baby to the clinic instead of having a vet come to us. I didn't want to risk a house call that resulted in having to take her there anyway. Double trauma for both of us. Scott used to care for the pets at home. He took them to the clinic only when necessary. He was the vet, it was his clinic, and this was his job. This time it was all me. Me who incompetently attempted to put the cage together until Mike took over. Me who had to sneak up on Baby and snatch her from her special safe spot. Me who had to clean the pee off the floor because she got so scared when she realized what was happening. Me who had to stuff her into a kennel designed for a St. Bernard because I couldn't have gotten her through the door of the cat-sized one. Me who had to sit in the back seat with her while Mike drove. Finally, me who had to turn my back and leave my terrified little girl all by herself. I sobbed pretty much from the time I made the decision to take her, until the time Mike and I dropped her off at the clinic Scott and I built - our clinic where I became just another customer when he did what he did.

It was good news, just a bladder infection, treated with an injection. Whew.

Mike and I worked on moving him into his room, unpacking the boxes he brought with him from Chicago, and finding places for his things. My plan was to go through Scott's room to try to make some space. I only got as far as opening his closet door and it was too much. It smells like him in there. Guess I'm not ready to address his clothing yet. Mike understands and is kindly living off the floor until I can make some room for him next weekend. I've asked Randy and Hunter to come over to help me sort through the tons of hunting gear I don't know what to do with. Bags and bags and closets of it.

Seems like a lot of two steps forward and one step back. Some days are even one step forward, two steps back. It's a very slow way to make any progress. I haven't been listening to JO or praying as much as I was. I think it's having an impact.

I think some of it is I'm feeling bad about Neil discouraging me from pursuing the home care business. Perhaps taking a timeout for now is not really a bad idea, but it was giving me something to think about and work on to keep myself busy. Now I have more free time to think about what has happened.

June 14, 2015

Uncle Kracker, Drift Away. It's the first song I've been able to listen to since the big day. I'm not sure why, but I've had zero interest in music. When I turned on JO today, there was a different preacher on his station. He was a bit aggressive for my taste so I started flipping around looking for a different Christian channel. Ran across Uncle K and actually wasn't disgusted by listening to singing. In fact, I made it really loud and even enjoyed it. Baby steps. I've even started eyeballing the latest Harlen Coben book that's been sitting on my table since my brother finished it several weeks ago. I used to read a new novel each week.

Now I don't have enough concentration to sit and read anything more than magazines and news. Just one more aspect of my life the f....er modified in a less than desirable way.

I told Karen about the discouragement I felt after talking with Neil about my home care plans. She reminded me I've said I could never thank him for everything he's done. She suggested I can thank him by putting my plans on hold for now and focusing on working for him. Let things settle down, help him with his business, then start thinking about the next step later. It's logical. She's right, of course. I think I'm hanging on to it because it's giving me hope - a future to strive for. Like maybe not ALL of my future is destroyed, just all of it except that.

Baby has forgiven me a full two weeks before I expected her to. Listening to her purr is so relaxing.

June 15, 2015

From the beginning of this mess, mornings have been bad. I always wake up feeling down. Some describe this as having a weight on their shoulders. Everyone has those random down days, but in this case my body wakes up in this state every morning. I remember during the first week Karen observed mornings were particularly hard for me. The positive thing is, what were once sitting-in-the-corner-crying-mornings, are now only generally blah.

I don't know when and how to discontinue the sleeping medication. Probably should call the doctor tomorrow for guidance. I would imagine just stopping altogether is not a good plan, even though the dose I'm on is very small. Could they be causing my morning blues?

June 16, 2015

The meeting with Neil and Earl the accountant went well. Poor Earl was so nervous, I think he thought I was upset with him and was bringing Neil in as back up. Not the case at all. I simply haven't been involved with the finances so it's all new to me. Neil was there to understand my situation so he can work with me long enough for me to get a handle on things.

During the meeting, Neil and Earl were talking about how Scott was such an entrepreneur and was always working on new things. I wanted to say "uh hello guys, those were my ideas. I was the planner and Scott the doer." We were a great team but neither one of us could've done what we did without the other. I was good at creating a game plan, not at carrying it out. That was him. I don't know if I'll have the courage to carry out any of my ideas without him helping and providing motivation and encouragement.

June 17, 2015

Most of the time, I haven't been able to identify reasons for bad days. Today I know. Two things happened to contribute. 1) one of the instructors asked for time off to take his wife to the hospital for a procedure. 2) Randy told me he'll be going for a colonoscopy tomorrow and may not be able to do a flight I've scheduled for him. Both situations involve medical procedures requiring someone to drive the other person home from the hospital. The person who was supposed to drive me home is no longer here. He left. I have no one to take care of me when a medical situation arises. Wasn't a Red X day but another depressing reminder of how alone in the world I am.

I ended up not going to group because I simply didn't want to. That's it, no other reason. Just didn't feel like going. Instead I went shopping for lots of fresh vegetables and the one item no house should ever be devoid of, cheesy Doritos. I made dinner, took it to the couch, then sat watching America's Got Talent while I ate my salad and garlic bread.

June 18, 2015

So much of the life I enjoyed is gone…so many things I don't enjoy have been added. Our silly jokes together, money and time to take awesome vacations, someone to prepare dinner when I'm tired, someone to pay the bills, a voice to call when I need a little support no matter how dumb, reading in bed while he watched the news, getting to fold his shirts and boxers, someone to deal with the house maintenance, a partner to scheme and plan our future with, a body to hug just because, someone to see smile when I come home with ice cream, the list is never ending. The more I realize, the more depressing it gets.

Mornings seem to be getting worse. I think it's the dreams. They're not nightmares like before, now they're just depressing. In last night's dream, I was wandering on a distant road and knew I needed to get home. I also knew it was miles away. I didn't know where my car was so I started walking but got lost. Finally, I found a bus and got on. I didn't know where it was going but I didn't want to keep walking. Same theme, different story. Alone. No one to call. Feeling of being on my own. Having to make my way through life with no one to help. Not knowing where I'm going. Same, same, same.

Even a happy dream, which is very rare, melts into the reality my life has become as soon as I wake up. A f......d up mess of drugs, loneliness, sadness, groups, counselors, overwhelming number of tasks to take care of each day, money concerns, and a general lack of excitement about the future. It's truly incomprehensible he did this to me. Perhaps I should feel sorry for him, for the future he lost, but I can't bring myself to have any compassion or understanding right now.

June 19, 2015

The more it goes the more it blows. There's a daily crappy surprise like a big pile of poop in a diaper. Surprise, time to clean up more mess. It seems like I spend every free moment managing paperwork. Poop pile today? "Escrow shortages." The county "reassessed" and the taxes are going up. I owe them money. Crap.

186

Trying to figure out how to cover all expenses on one income is challenging. Funny how Scott thought we'd be fine with just one. I wonder if he was a bit overly optimistic and saw what he wanted to see. I should have gotten involved in the finances a long time ago. I'm telling my married friends to write instructions for each other in the event one passes away. It will make it so much easier on the survivor.

Mike starts his job on Monday. I'm hopeful, but a little pessimistic, he'll be able to maintain a full-time work schedule. He hasn't been able to for years. Based on his work ethic around the house, I have my doubts. I sincerely hope he can pull it together.

Therapist's reflections:

Missy begins to notice mornings are particularly difficult for her. There's a heaviness, or sadness, magnified during this time of day. It's not uncommon, three months out, to start noticing a certain time of day is more challenging than others. You're slowly moving out of the protective fog into a place where everything feels exposed and unbearable. You're developing a routine. A part of this new routine may be a trigger time. For some, it's after work when their loved one should be walking in the door and discussing their day with them. For others this trigger time is after dinner, when there's quiet and downtime. The mind plays the movie reel of our loved one's death. And of their absence.

What is your trigger time? Is there a time of day more uncomfortable than others? Learn to anticipate this time. It could be a certain couple of hours, or it could be as soon as the sun sets - or rises in Missy's case. Learn to accept it. You don't need to run from it. Once you've identified your trigger time, you can begin to plan your days accordingly to make it easier on yourself. If you know night time is difficult, don't plan business meetings, or activities in which you'll need to be mentally alert. During these difficult times, avoid complex and difficult activities. When you feel so much is out of your control, doing these small things can help you slowly begin to take back control.

What I noticed in Missy during this time:

The little things that once went unnoticed are now like neon signs flashing in Missy's eyes. The permanence of Scott's absence has set in. The absence of the little things now takes center stage. The missing phone calls and texts. Quiet evenings spent watching television together. Noticing it was Scott who called the electric company when there was an issue with the monthly bill. Or replaced the water filter in the refrigerator when necessary. This is an important element of loss often discounted by others. These little acts equated to love, consistency, and security in her relationship with Scott. When one small act was missing, it was a big void in her daily life.

Chapter 14

The Thirteenth Week

Today is your day!
Your mountain is waiting.
So get on your way!

Dr. Seuss

Looking back:

What I see in this week is the woman reaching the conclusion it's time to clean up the mess. She must fully accept this conclusion before she can begin to make meaningful progress. She's actively formulating a plan, making lists, and even making some tiny changes. Although she's weary from her three-month journey, she's feeling a bubble of energy building within her. It's a feeling she hasn't experienced for quite some time. She feels fortunate to have people around her who are not willing to coddle her. Their feedback sometimes hurts and makes her cringe, but she realizes their guidance is beneficial. She listens to them. Coddling works with her at times, but she understands too much is detrimental to her quest to move forward. This week, to her horror, she curiously peeked in the window of the new egg store as she walked by. It felt wrong, but she did it anyway.

What I know now:

- If you recognize certain days of the week are more difficult than others, have a plan to do something nice on those days.
- You might notice yourself doing spacey things you've never done before. Just laugh when this happens, you'll get back to your normal self. Later, when you reflect on this time, you'll be amused at some of the things you did.
- If you notice you're making progress and moving forward, BE OK WITH IT. I can't say for sure, but sometimes it seemed some survivors I met resisted progress and becoming ok again, as if it was disrespectful to the deceased. I wondered if they were doing what they thought others expected them to do...look sad and feel miserable. If you feel good, be good!
- Think about ways to make your life easier, about little changes you can make. Big changes are probably better left for later.
- Sometimes friends who will give you "tough love" aren't such a bad thing.
- Every now and then take an inventory of all the things going well in your life. Say thank you for them. Do it out loud.

June 20, 2015

Question: Where am I going? Answer: I don't know but I'm not staying here.

June 21, 2015

Two red X days in a row. Saturday and Sunday. Saturday was an avalanche of the extreme number of tasks needing to be done every day. From the minute I woke up until the minute I went to bed, both days were spent trying to catch my breath. Yesterday was Saturday, this is how it went…wake up, feed the pets, take a shower, clean the litter boxes, clean up cat puke, walk outside to get the newspaper, eat breakfast while making a list of banking items needing my attention, try to get some of them done, wash the dishes, do laundry, file business documents, go shopping, catch and release yet another lizard the cats brought in the house, give the dogs a few minutes of attention, call the yard guy because the grass is getting yellow, look on the city of Chandler website to try to figure out why my water bill jumped $50, put the bill in the car to remember to call on Monday, go to the storage unit office to give them my new credit card number, calculate what to do with a rental house that's not generating income (stupid "assessment" and tax increase), call to schedule a meeting with the property manager to discuss the problem house, handle a couple of calls from the instructors, try to figure out why Scott's 401K seems to have vanished from my accounting system. This is not an exaggeration, and all while my mind was already on today, Sunday, the day Hunter and Randy came over to help me go through some of Scott's hunting gear.

That didn't go so well either. I was able to give up some of his things but ended up holding on to most. Three new pair of size 14 hiking boots…not sure why I'm keeping those, an entire large duffle bag full of hunting attire I can't bring myself to even look at yet, and over ten hunting knives. What a waste of a life.

I finally got around to eating lunch at four. It was then, while I was eating and concurrently sorting two years of tax documents...making a lame attempt to organize them for delivery to the storage unit, that I lost it. It occurred to me I was stuffing the entire life we built together into duffle bags and boxes so they could sit on a shelf, in a dark storage unit. Everything...his hobbies that were so much a part of him, the businesses we created together, mementos, pictures...all in boxes. I've barely scratched the surface of going through his things to decide what to do with them. It was just too much. I hit a breaking point on the way to the storage unit for the second time that day.

On the drive home, I pulled over behind a grocery store where the deliveries come and go and called Karen in hysterics. Her feedback was pretty hard to hear. She said, "Yes, your life has changed but there are ways to simplify." I know, but so much changed in such a short period of time. Even though I know she's right, it's still hard to hear someone else say it. I think I can eventually get it all under control, but right now, it feels like I'm trying to climb the Himalayas barefoot wearing a swimsuit - completely exposed and facing an impossible task.

June 22, 2015

Well now I've done it. Not even three months have gone by and I've already checked out a Christian dating site. Totally wrong on every level but things just can't stay the way they are. Looking shows me there are options. This might not be the right option for me, but I like to know all possibilities. It helps my brain organize things and gives me a little peace. It gives me a little hope my current situation won't be this way forever. If I was stuck here, it would be intolerable.

Mike started his new job today. He won't be able to take the dogs to the clinic any longer. It's where they're used to spending their days. One more problem to solve. Their routine will be disrupted which will create something else for me to worry about. Worry, worry, worry. Maybe I could hire a neighbor kid to drive them back and forth. Maybe I could hire someone to worry for me.

Buying a Father's Day card for my dad was tough. There was a "For Husband" section. One more reminder I no longer have a husband...just having to read that word...

June 23, 2015

Stagnant. Hollow. Losing the fire. Tired. Those are some of the adjectives Jill used to describe me in our session today. Yikes, ouch, not true. Yes, absolutely true. The first two, stagnant and hollow, bother me the most. The last one, tired, doesn't. The fact is, I'm doing many things that are very emotional, many that are only task oriented...all of them very draining. All on less sleep than I am used to. It's time to get back in the game. It's what JO said the other day, shake off the discouragement and self-pity and get back in the game. He said it's easy to stay in faith when times are good, very difficult when they're not. He also said, if you move forward, God will turn your scars into stars for His glory.

It's time to escort discouragement and self-pity to the door and move forward. It's time to do what I always do. Make a plan.

June 24, 2015

Being emotionally tired is much more draining than being physically tired. It's time to think logically. What is so emotionally draining? What recharges my batteries? These things must be explored before I can begin to solve the Stagnant, Hollow, Losing the Fire, Tired problem, hereafter known as the S.H.I.T. problem. You have to imagine the "L" looks like an "I" to make the acronym work. Minor detail... Anyone who's experienced a traumatic loss realizes details and perfection lose value as quickly as a bad day on Wall Street. Besides, it's my acronym so I can call it whatever I want. It's decided. Operation De-S.H.I.T.

Speaking of details, it was interesting to have lunch with Suzanne today. She's three months ahead of me in this process. It was her husband also. We laughed about the stupid things we do now we didn't used to. Let's just say we're having some very blonde moments. My thing has been forgetting to hook my belt after going to the bathroom. In the last month, I've done it about five times. I don't ever remember doing it in the past. I even walked through an entire restaurant and sat down with both ends

194

of my belt hanging down. What's up with that? Walking from the living room to the bedroom to get something and forgetting what I was looking for by the time I get there. Leaving things in unusual places that require a detective to find them. Driving away from the gas station with the gas nozzle still plugged into my car. Then there was the time I buttoned my shorts, got the belt together but forgot the zipper. Fortunately…really fortunately, I discovered it as I walked down the hall…on my way to speak in front of a group of people.

Anyway, back to deploying Operation De-S.H.I.T.

Step 1: Define the problem.
Step 2: Design a fix for the problem.
Step 3: Apply the fix.
Step 4: Evaluate the results.
Step 5: Make any necessary changes to Step 2.

This might take a few days so this entry may end up being a multiday entry. I might actually have to go back and read something I wrote…that would be a first.

Step 1 – Define the Problem. I'm feeling physically and emotionally drained.
Step 2 – Design a Fix for the Problem. Ideas:
- Read the bible more, even if only a random paragraph each day.
- Only go to the mail box one time per week. Friday would be good.
- Set aside a day for doing all bills at one time to minimize the stress. Saturday or Sunday.

- Make going to the gym at least four times per week a priority.
- Get my butt to bed no later than ten.
- Go back to listening JO every day.
- Make an effort to talk to one friend per week about the status of my progress. Hard one!
- Stop worrying about Mike and eventually make a plan to set some expectations.
- Make more effort to check on others and how they're doing.

Step 3 - Apply the fix. Ready, set, GO. Start tomorrow.

June 26, 2015

Today was kind of funky. Not funky like 70's music, Farrah Fawcett hair, and Hash Jeans with a beaded star on the butt. Funky as in I was in a funk, not happy. Is it because it's the 26th? Friday? Both days have significance now. Hard to say.

I think the scale that weighs the benefits vs. disadvantages of having Mike living with me may be tipping a bit. Not in his favor. Today was the end of his first week on his job. I understand he needs to settle in and figure out his schedule. It's ok that he's not able to drop the dogs off and pick them up from the clinic every day. What I'm not ok with was his response to my text asking if he was planning to pick them up… "Just leaving work now I'm going to go straight to the course and hit some range balls so will be home later." Um, ok. So…you've still paid absolutely squat toward any expenses and now you're going to drive the truck (ie dog transport vehicle) I've

196

given you to drive, on my insurance, to the golf course instead of picking up the dogs?!?! Wow. I'm trying to be fair but he seems to be doing less and less to help. He knows picking them up in the car I drive is difficult. Perhaps Tina was right when she called me a "sugar mama."

The problem is when you negotiate, you have to be willing to walk away. I'm not quite ready to have him leave so I don't think it's time to negotiate. I'll give it another week to see how it goes before I consider asking him to get his own car. Then I can drive the truck and take care of the dogs myself.

What does he do to contribute? Take out the garbage occasionally, empty the dishwasher, pick up dog poop, bring in the garbage and recycle bin, feed the pets when he's up before me. Other benefits of having him here? A potential person to go out to eat or to a movie with on the weekend, a reluctant church buddy, someone to say good morning to, someone to watch TV with at night, a body in the house so it doesn't feel so empty. That last one feels very important.

What would make me feel better about him being here? A better plan for the dogs, financial contribution. I guess that's all I can think of so maybe after he gets another week of his new job under his belt we can talk, perhaps even resolve those two issues.

De-S.H.I.T. report for the day. All tasks accomplished except getting to bed before ten and worrying about Mike's presence... did it.

JO wisdom for the day: 1) Take what you have and make the most of it. 2) Finish the following sentence with what you want to be, not what you think you are. "I am..." Or as I've heard before, dress for the job you want, not the job you have. My "I am's..." for the day:

- I am blessed.
- I am happy.
- I am peaceful.
- I am going to have an awesome future.
- I am loved.
- I am strong.
- I am courageous.
- I am going to successfully take charge of my financial future.
- I am going to make good decisions by myself.
- I am capable of handling everything.

I think his point is to say these things until I believe them.

Therapist's reflections:

For many Survivors, cleaning out a loved one's possession can be daunting, and tricky. There's a real urge to move forward, and redesigning your personal space is one way to do this. With the urge comes guilt, the feeling that by removing your loved one's things, you're in some way leaving them behind, forgetting them. It's another decision that may feel as if there's no clear answer.

I always suggest the process of cleaning out, giving away, or purging your loved one's items be a SLOW one. After all, this is one of the things you DO have control over at the moment. Your life may feel full of regrets, don't add more to the list by cleaning things out before you're ready.

Deciding when to deal with your loved one's things is an individual choice. There's really no right or wrong timing. Some Survivors may begin this clean out only a few months after the death, others may not be ready for several years. Listen to your gut, even if it doesn't align with the advice others are giving you.

During this time, you may be able to look back and see how far you've come, how much has already changed for you in a short period of time. The pain is still intense, and your eggs are still broken, but the effort you've put into self-care is proving to work. Not that you like it, but you're able to stand on your own. Maybe you're driving now instead of relying on others to get you where you need to go. Maybe you're beginning to re-engage socially (as difficult as it feels). You're beginning to do more on your own, without the everyday support of others.

It's important to stop and take stock of where you've been, and what you've been able to overcome thus far. Take note of your successes, big or small, as this is important to your confidence. Missy did this by writing in her journal. At times when she thought she was standing still and not making progress, she could have looked back through her journal to see where she was a short time ago. In Missy's case, she wasn't comfortable revisiting her entries, instead she sent them to me. In our work together, I would remind her of where she had been and what she'd already overcome. If you aren't a journaler, find someone in your life you trust to point out these accomplishments. Progress is also easy to gauge when you're part of a support group. Being three months out from your loss and sitting across the room from someone who is three weeks out, will remind you of how much progress you've made.

What I noticed in Missy during this time:

Missy was emotionally lower than she'd been in previous weeks, she felt helpless. She was unable to snap her fingers and reconfigure her life. She was uncertain of what her future held. She realized, maybe for the first time, she wasn't in control over her grief as much as she thought she would be.

Missy walked into this trauma with an "I'll show you" attitude. She was mentally strong and driven before Scott's death. A real go-getter. After Scott's suicide, she was shocked and limping, but figured she could flex her muscles, dig deep, and take control of this grief, like she had most other obstacles in her life.

At this stage Missy was indifferent and complacent to counseling. She didn't want to hear her grief was "normal." She wanted immediate change: a new life, love, partner, and prosperity, without putting in the time and hard work needed to gain those new things. Missy needed tough love.

Chapter 15

Looking Back on the First Three Months

Keep going. That's all you have to do, ever.
You really don't have to be amazing,
Or fierce or beautiful
Or successful or good.
Just keep going please.
Slowly is fine. Crawling is fine.
No feeling is final.
Except hope.

Glennon Doyle

Which emotional can of worms would be opened? It was this concern that kept me from re-reading any part of my journal until three years after Scott died. Cautiously, and with nerves flaring, I finally felt brave enough to take a peek. As with many things throughout this process, the anticipation was much worse than the actual event.

In many ways, it was like reading someone else's story. Some of it entertained me, some made me cringe, a couple of times I almost cried. It all made me realize how awful that time was, how far I've traveled, and the size of the village it took to push, pull, drag, and carry me to this point. My thinking was scattered, the anger I felt over-ruled much of my emotion, and the desperation I felt contaminated nearly everything I said or did. Even though most of the first year, and certainly the three months contained herein, was a complete fog, I remember nearly everything. It seems like just yesterday my husband killed himself. At the same time, it seems like a lifetime ago.

As I re-read the entries, the person I see in the journal entries is not the person I was before he died. Nor is she the person I am today. During that time, some difficult truths about myself were not only exposed, they were exaggerated. Extreme pressure does that, I supposed. My angry was angrier, my needy was rendered helpless, and it some ways my weaknesses were my strengths. They all helped me survive. I thought, said, and wrote things that were extremely harsh. For this book they remain as written at that time for the purpose of showing how my mind was working in those moments...how another survivor's mind might be working also.

Engulfing the angry, the sad, the hateful, the helplessness, and everything else, was a London-thick fog. Through this fog, none of these truths could be seen for what they were. Not by me. Not then. Now, as I reflect back, I can see that time for what it was. The truths I was living are clearer. During the first three months, life turned back to a time before I'd learned even the most basic of skills. I existed on instincts and caveman-like survival skills. Wake up, do what it took to live through one more day, go to sleep. Only the things most critical to human survival were present. Many days, even those were absent.

I recall only two times the fog turned into an impenetrable dark night... complete blackness with not even a pinhole of light coming through to lead me in the direction of healing. The first occurred about two weeks after he died. Driving home from a Survivors of Suicide meeting with friend, I recall sitting in her passenger seat, feeling completely hopeless. Like I was completely covered by a pile of wet, heavy, dirt. I remember thinking "there's no way out." It's a feeling I've never forgotten. The second time was not much later…it happened when I walked out of my garage one day and was passing the fig tree Scott and I planted. Barely clothed, I stopped on the hot pavers which were burning by feet, put my hands on my knees and thought I didn't care if I died. Killing myself was never an option, but I do recall at that moment, I didn't care if it happened. Besides those two brief moments, I always had hope, I always knew I'd keep going. What I didn't know was how happy my life would turn out. In those three months, I didn't believe it was possible.

The first three months, recorded in Book One of this Frantic Series, can be understood by visualizing a large fish, freshly thrown on shore…a foreign and hostile territory. She lies there gasping for air, flopping frantically against the rocks and sand. Trying to find her way back into the water.

Months four through six, are recorded in Part Two of the series, Frantic Caged. During this time the fish lies still as a crowd gathers to figure out how to rescue her. The fish is no longer flailing, but still not able to breath. Perhaps she has confidence the crowd will save her. More likely, she's run out of energy and is conserving what she has remaining.

Part Three, Frantic Tamed, is a record of the rest of the first year (months seven through twelve). The crowd gently places the fish back into the water and holds her upright. She is still weak, unable to do anything except hover in the current as oxygen enters her gills. She's severely disabled and struggling but on the way to recovering. She just needs to sit quietly for a while, watching the events around her, as her strength to continue swimming is gathered. She has deep scars from the day she was thrown to the shore, they make her much stronger. The fish is a survivor.

If you've read this far, you're a survivor too.

To attempt to provide others with a blueprint for survival would be futile. Things helpful to me may not work for others. It's my sincerest hope survivors who read this will gain a small boost in their recovery process. I also hope those around survivors gain some insight to the reality the survivor may be living…and in turn, be able to play a positive part in the healing process.

I can identify three things critical to my survival; my unwavering faith God had a plan; friends and family who gathered to gently escort me back into the water and keep me alive until I could begin to fend for myself; and the resources that came my way. My resources included a counselor who remains by my side even today, the available community services, and other Survivors to provide hope that one day I would be able to breathe and laugh again.

Since Scott's death, I've been blessed with the opportunity to support others who reached out to me after suffering a loss to suicide. I learned a long time ago that being on the other side, part of the support system, is just as difficult as being the survivor. The survivor is not the only one who walks blindly through the mess. So do those around them. We don't know what to say, what do to, or how to act. As I provide support to others, I try to remember what helped me most during this time.

When it comes down to it, I guess the thing that helped the most was the time people gave me. The time they took to sit and listen until I was all cried out, the time they took in the morning to send a text, to call just to see how I was doing, to help me overcome an obstacle I'd encountered, to attend groups or doctor's appointments with me, to let me know they cared and were thinking about me. That's it, just their time. The gifts were nice, the advice they offered was well intended, the meals provide were helpful...but the time they shared was by far the most valuable thing anyone gave me. Whether they knew it or not, they were doing exactly what Jill suggested in the very beginning...they were acting as my bubble wrap as I healed.

Recently, when I was touring Gibraltar, something interesting occurred to me. The town is a mix of very old and brand new. Much of it was destroyed by wars throughout the decades, much of it has been rebuilt. The town feels jumbled, crumbling walls surround the city, the colors around the town don't match, the streets aren't straight, the population is diverse, and the monkeys roam freely. If Scott was here we would laugh about how cute they are, and in very pathetic French accents, call them "minkies." It's something we heard Peter Sellers say about 22 years ago in a Pink Panther movie. It was one of our inside jokes.

It occurred to me my life is my own little Gibraltar. When the bomb of Scott's suicide hit, much of my life collapsed. Just like Gibraltar. The stronger areas survived, others did not. But they've been rebuilt. My life is now a mix of the old and the new...just like Gibraltar. The landscape is different now, it's been patched back together, and it works quite well. So will yours.

The only advice (and I use that term loosely) I can offer survivors is to surround yourself with supportive people, keep taking one more breath, keep putting one foot in front of the other. Celebrate successfully doing these things when you can. Sometimes this will mean celebrating 60 seconds of survival, later your first cry-free day, and eventually, finding something in your life that's not only returned to the way it was, but is even better. And that's just the beginning if you keep going. Keep working. Keep having hope.

Resources

Suicide Prevention and Suicide Support Resource Guide:
If you or anybody you know needs help, below is a list of National Services for your reference.

National Suicide Prevention Lifeline
https://suicidepreventionlifeline.org
1800-273-8255

Kevin's Song
http://kevinssong.org
313-236-7109

American Association of Suicidology
http://www.suicidology.org
202-237-2280

National Action Alliance for Suicide Prevention
http://actionallianceforsuicideprevention.org
 202-223-4059

American Foundation for Suicide Prevention
https://afsp.org
212-363-3500

The Jed Foundation
https://www.jedfoundation.org
 212-647-7544

Suicide Prevention Resource Center http://www.sprc.org/
877-438-7772
Survivors of Suicide
http://www.survivorsofsuicide.com/

Veterns Crisis Line
www.veteranscrisisline.net
1-800-273-8255

Author Biography

Missy grew up in Idaho with her siblings, Karen and Mike. She received a basketball scholarship to play for four years at Tulane University. In 1988, while studying for her Master's Degree at Oregon State University, she met Scott McComb. They married in 1991. Missy got a job working as a parole officer in  Oregon shortly after graduation, although life was determined to take her elsewhere.

In 1997, she began taking helicopter lessons and completed her certifications and ratings one year later. She began working for Quantum Helicopters in 1998 where she has been the Chief Flight Instructor since 2000.

Life can throw anyone a curveball, and that's exactly what happened to Missy. On March 27th, 2015, Missy's husband died by Suicide. Missy has learned the value of life is much more than degrees, accomplishments, and titles after your name. The fragmentation of her perfect world that smashed all the eggs she had so perfectly lined up in her basket, is proof that what appears to be perfect, can be broken.

Therapist Biography
Jill is a licensed professional counselor who has focused on working with Survivors of Suicide and generalized grief since 2003. She was first introduced to those bereaved by suicide while working for The Wendt Center for Loss and Healing in Washington, D.C. Jill knew almost immediately that  she wanted to focus her life's work on helping Survivors. She appreciates the uniqueness and dispelling of the social stigma associated with this grief. Her goal is to provide a safe space for those struggling with loss and to help provide hope for those feeling confused, helpless and alone.

Jill provides local training on both prevention and postvention. She and a co-speaker have been invited to speak at the American Association of Suicidology national conference on several occasions, as well as the Canadian Association for Suicide Prevention conference two years in a row. Jill has also spoken at the International Association for Suicide Prevention conference in Oslo, Norway, and Talin, Estonia. Providing education through community presentations happens to be one of her favorite things to do.

Education
Colorado State University:
Graduated with a degree in Liberal Arts, 1993
University of Colorado-Denver:
Graduated with a Master's Degree in Counseling Psychology, 2003.

Links

https://franticbooks.com/

https://www.facebook.com/franticbooks/

franticbookseries@gmail.com

11922871R10129

Made in the USA
Middletown, DE
15 November 2018